W9-DEI-431

Branding Only Works on Cattle

Branding Only Works on Cattle

The New Way to Get Known

(and drive your competitors crazy)

Jonathan Salem Baskin

**BUSINESS
PLUS**

NEW YORK   BOSTON

Business Plus
Hachette Book Group USA
237 Park Avenue
New York, NY 10017
Visit our Web site at www.HachetteBookGroupUSA.com.

Business Plus is an imprint of Grand Central Publishing.
The Business Plus name and logo are trademarks of
Hachette Book Group USA, Inc.

Printed in the United States of America

First Edition: September 2008

10 9 8 7 6 5 4 3 2 1

Library of Congress Cataloging-in-Publication Data

Baskin, Jonathan Salem.
    Branding only works on cattle: the new way to get known *(and drive your competitors crazy)* / Jonathan Salem Baskin.
        p. cm.
    ISBN-13: 978-0-446-17801-3
    ISBN-10: 0-446-17801-2
    1. Branding (Marketing) 2. Consumer behavior. 3. Information behavior.
4. Internet searching. 5. Business enterprises—Computer network resources.
I. Title.

HF5415.1255.B37 2008
658.8'27—dc22

                                                                    2007034391

ISBN 978-0-446-54077-3 (international pbk.)

For Cate

Acknowledgments

Many people contributed to this book.

I've shamelessly quoted, borrowed, adapted, modified, and sometimes misunderstood ideas and experiences from folks who are smarter, more successful, and far more enlightened than I am. The conclusions I present herein are my own, but if I got things right, it's thanks to their great counsel. If I'm wrong on something, blame me.

I want to thank Peter Baskin, my brother, for his many contributions, as well as acknowledge Ron Belanger, Antonio Bertone, Jonah Bloom, Susan Boland, Jerry Bowles, danah boyd, Lincoln Briggs, Jimmy Brown, Alex Chisholm, David Churbuck, Brian Clark, Paul Coletta, Robbie Cooper, Katie Cotton, Richard Cutting, George Doigami, Ryan Eckel, Mike Fasulo, Carl Folta, Tammi Franke, Richard Getler, Brian Giamo, Kimberly Greenberger, Chaim Guggenheim, Eric Hiss, Hideo Hohgi, Cynthia Holladay, Paula Hoppe, Richard Horne, Holly Houk, Paul Jackson, Henry Jenkins, Brian Kardon and his entire team at Forrester Research, Inc., Mark Karnes, Tom Katzenmeyer, Paul Kedrosky, Jennifer Kirk, Robert Khoo, Peter Kim, Kurt Koepfle, Richard Kohn, Stuart Krauskopf, Jim Lenskold, Karyl

Levinson, Charlene Li, Lisa Long, Craig MacDonald, Jean-Marie Maier, Heather Meeker, Grant McCracken, Craig Merrigan, Ruth Mortimer, Randall Munroe, Ann Murray, Aki Noda, Reed Nolte, Jennifer O'Leary, Tom O'Toole, Florian Peter, Jean-Pascal Peyret, Larry Ponemon, Andy Rench, Sarah Robbins, Calli Robertson, Pamela Robertson, Douglas Rushkoff, Nancy Sagar, Daniel Savage, Ted Schadler, David M. Scott, Andy Sernovitz, Robert Sharp, Kallie Shimek, Mark Sims, Michael Smith, V. Srinivasan, Dawn Stanford, Dave Sutton, Dave Szulborski, David Taylor, Ilya Vedrashko, Greg Verdino, Helen Wade, Colleen Wainwright, Felix Warburg, Terry White, and Alex Wolfe.

I owe much to my agent, David Fugate of LaunchBooks Literary Agency, for his expertise and goodwill in helping transform my dream about a book into something real. I was very lucky to work with Rick Wolff, editorial director at Grand Central Publishing/Business Plus, whose supportive, insightful guidance made sure my dream didn't turn into a nightmare.

Finally, I have the good fortune to belong to a family of thinkers who act on their beliefs, dreamers who strive to make their hopes real, and people who don't just talk about love, but show it. Starting when I was little more than a speck, my parents taught me that no action was ever too small to take, and no accomplishment too inconsequential to celebrate, as long as the behavior originated in sincere, thoughtful intent.

I hope I have made them as proud of me as I am of them.

Contents

Challenging Ptolemy's Imagination

It was late last century. I was interviewing for a job running user interface design for a firm that integrated the computer software that companies were buying at the time. One of the interviewers asked me to name a website I thought was particularly well-branded.

"Napster," I quickly answered.

She sighed. "Umm, that's an application, not a website."

Thanks, you unctuous snot, I thought. Napster would soon boast 70 million subscribers worldwide, heralding the file sharing phenomenon, iTunes, and an ongoing restructuring of the entire entertainment industry. Instant messaging, a Napster-like gizmo for conversation, would attract 150 million plus users, and become part of the tool set transforming businesses worldwide.

I was intrigued that Napster had been branded by its functionality and relevance, not by a pretty ad or a textbook definition. Yet my interviewer wanted to bicker over the right label.

Little did I know that we'd be similarly paralyzed in our understanding and approach to branding as our new century matures into its teens.

You and I live in a world bombarded by Napster's prolific progeny: websites, online services, media outlets and devices, and more ways to create, share, modify, and enjoy just about anything that can be expressed in a digital format.

As consumers, we're faced with ever more choices that make ever less obvious sense to us. We shop, interact, contemplate, and make decisions differently than we did in the dark ages of the 1900s. As businesspeople, we strive to find ways around this chaos, and to somehow use branding to connect again directly with our customers and consumers.

There's no shortage of advice on how to do it.

Books, learned papers, and pop magazine articles relentlessly tout the latest branding idea, usually outdating the last one you're still trying to implement. Consultants create slide presentations to spin the chaos into projects for which you can pay. Another generation of college dropouts always seem to show up with some incomprehensibly innovative technology that will answer all of your branding challenges with the push of a button.

And forget the fancy stuff: how about those brochures that have to be a certain color, or the PR talking points that favor one adjective over another. Or all of those meetings and expenditures and time spent branding because, well, it's just what you're supposed to do.

Labels. Definitions. The "right" way to do things.

You know what I'm talking about. It has never added up or truly made sense. You've probably recently read a book on brands as sexual pheromones or quantum moments between clicks on social network sites, hired gurus who express your brand as a glowing stalagmite, or maybe bought a new technology tool that reads people's minds, or something.

But I'd wager you haven't found the answer yet.

That's because there's still this big ugly not-so-secret secret that we marketers dance around. Everyone senses it, but nobody feels comfortable addressing the questions that should inevitably follow.

Branding doesn't work anymore.

We can't buy our way around this fact. No blog, chat room, or buzz marketing campaign will do it, and it isn't reasonable to expect that we can sit back and watch consumers produce ads and then sell to themselves. We can't overcome this reality by being funnier or edgier, or deciding to name it something or another.

People just aren't doing what we once believed they would do with brands.

We hold on to our habits, however, because the traditional benefits of branding—awareness, preference, loyalty—are certainly desirable goals. But every time you ask a question about your brand, you usually get definitions, ideas, and plans that seem so right, yet inevitably prove to be so wrong or just incomplete.

You need another brilliant branding solution like you need a hole in the head.

Branding doesn't work anymore, and before you read the next gee-whiz book, hire a consultant, or buy a technological gizmo, maybe you should stop trying to come up with answers and instead start asking different questions.

Maybe it isn't enough to talk about how to brand anymore, but rather *if* it's reasonable to expect to brand at all. Further, if there's a different way to conceive of brands, are there better, different ways to deliver them?

Branding Only Works on Cattle asks these questions, and then proposes a number of possible answers that I hope will prompt more discovery and help identify even better solutions.

That's easier said than done, however.

Lots of smart, erudite people are dedicated to preserving the status quo. Billions of dollars, jobs, IPOs, and entire businesses depend on companies buying the next Big Branding Thing in response to asking the same old questions in the same old ways. We're well into a second generation of marketers who grew up in a world defined by the habits of branding's mid-twentieth-century heyday.

So asking marketers to answer the question about brands is kind of like asking mental patients to assess and prescribe their own therapy. I should know, because I've been one of the inmates.

This is where you come in.

The impact of change on how we envision and deliver branding is just too big and substantive to be left to the marketers alone. Whether you're in operations, human resources, or finance, or are an independent contractor, an art historian, a regular ol' consumer, a bon vivant about town or, yes, a marketer, you can and must collaborate on answering the questions that have befuddled the best marketing minds of our times.

Branding doesn't work anymore, and you need to be part of a new approach to figuring out why, and then what to do about it.

Just saying such a thing is revolutionary. It almost feels crazy, doesn't it? That's why nobody likes to say it. Most folks would rather get the wrong answers than risk going out on a limb and trying to change the system.

But you're not most folks.

You want to break through this cycle of imperfect answers, and you're willing to take risks and extend yourself in order to get past that brick wall of habit, defensiveness, and budget control. You already sense that the challenge facing brands may not be a tactical issue, solvable by the latest technology contrivance or marketing fad.

You know that our latest solutions will fail to solve this problem because our problem is how we've been trying to solve it.

Branding doesn't work anymore, and we need to ask *is it possible that we've just got it wrong?*

It's very possible. Just ask Ptolemy.

No, he's not some branding guru with his own consulting service for achieving oodles of brand whatever. Ptolemy lived around the second century, somewhere near Alexandria, Egypt, where he codified a model for understanding the entire cosmos—subsequently called the Ptolemaic system—in which the Earth was at the center of an ever more complex web of circles that guided the motion of celestial objects. Some of the circles intersected, others overlapped, and many circles were positioned within other circles. The system was brilliantly complicated, and when a new object was discovered, a new gear was added in order to explain it.

Though fathomable only to an ever smaller caste of the initiated, the Ptolemaic system predicted celestial motion with great accuracy. It was considered true by every man, woman, and child who lived during the next 1,500 years of human history.

But it was wrong.

Not just sort of wrong, but fundamentally, irrevocably, *oh-we-were-so-dumb* wrong.

The Earth is not at the center of the universe. The motion of celestial objects is rarely if ever a perfect circle. Why things move *across* the sky has nothing to do with the precision or interactions of gears. There's no *across* the sky, really, and the true laws that govern space and time should make our heads spin, let alone challenge the limits of Ptolemy's imagination.

So why did people believe it for so long? There are at least three broad reasons:

- **It worked, for the most part.** Remember, their technology amounted to candles and leeches, and beyond their backyards lurked a scary, infinite cosmos. The Ptolemaic system was a fairly accurate overlay that imposed order on apparent chaos. And it was so complicated that it was impossible for most people to question it, even when it didn't quite work.

- **Nobody wanted to prove it wrong anyway.** For centuries, everyone believed that the earth was the center of things, because they believed in their own special uniqueness among the animals of the earth and all the objects in space. As such, the institutions of society were conceived and managed to this purpose. So Ptolemy's system *fit*. Only experts could explain the system, and their job security depended on them preserving its relevance.

- **There wasn't a viable alternative.** Advances in technology and modeling made a challenge inescapable, but not for a long, long time. There was just no alternative for what was right, so there was no reason to prove it wrong.

After Copernicus, however, astronomers found new ways to describe planetary and stellar motion. Better telescopes revealed a cosmos too busy to be explained by Ptolemy's clockwork models. His best-seller parchments and zillion-step system were relegated to the cutout bin of history.

Ptolemy didn't work anymore.

Now, imagine for a moment the parallels to our approach to brands in business today:

- **It works, for the most part.** Sort of, and primarily because we don't really hold it accountable for much. Awareness helps sell things, no two ways about it, so we see circumstantial evidence of branding in our everyday lives. It's an easy explanation for things that defy easy explanation, and we generally look at it as an unavoidable, though unexplainable, cost of doing business.

- **Nobody wants to prove it wrong anyway.** There's an established, entrenched *Creative Media Industrial Complex*, with a vested financial interest in perpetuating the belief in brands, while selling the services that affirm it. Too many habits and job descriptions rely on keeping things just the way they are.

- **There's never been an alternative viewpoint.** Even though humanity functioned without allegiance to branding up until the twentieth century, we've assumed it's an incontrovertible fixture of life, irrespective of its constant failures and shortcomings. It's less science than art or religion, and faith in it allows believers to accommodate any and all evidence that might challenge it.

However, if you look at brands without the jaundiced eye of comfort and habit, you're in for a startling surprise: our traditional ideas have become empty labels, without meaning, rendering our branding activities inert and ineffective.

Branding doesn't work anymore.

I will argue that it's no longer adequate to see brands as based on what consumers *think*, as things that can be *presented* to the world, or as communications constructs with which people want to *interact*. This book is about a *reality phenomenon,* not just a business trend. And it's about finding things that we can do about it.

It's about exploring the common drivers of the changes we see impacting brands, whether this year or next. It's about going beyond the reactions to this change from people who hope to make money on it, and exploring the centrality of *behavior* in our lives—how the changes in our world have impacted the *who, what, where, when,* and *why* consumers and customers act—and only then applying it to the way we envision and deliver branding.

As such, the key to my line of questioning is to examine ways to *behave differently*, from how you conceive of your brand to how it's developed, delivered, and supported.

Branding doesn't work anymore, at least not generically, but it is working in novel, sometimes disparate activities around the world. Examples of new solutions are also coming from people across the enterprise—from any and every department—as well as from consumers, vendors, suppliers, friends, and critics.

This book is about what they're doing and thinking, and how you can apply their experience and conversations to your business: better use of online search; smarter endorsements and more productive customer relations; more compelling ads; websites and promotions with a purpose; clearer ways to evaluate what gets spent on branding, which also means there are ways to constantly improve it.

Since you've read this far, you're already a participant in the conversation. Finish the book, and you'll qualify as a true brand heretic, ready to shake the status quo down to its very brand vapors, molecules, or whatever nonsense your branding ptolemies have extracted from their imaginations.

In the end, you may disagree with elements of my case, quibble a factoid, or debate a conclusion. But there are two facts this book will establish:

1. The world has changed since the principles of branding were conceived. So using the same old guiding principles and hoping for different answers over and over again is a textbook definition of insanity, irrespective of how flashy or new the experiments appear to be.

2. We need to challenge Ptolemy's imagination, and invent instead a new philosophy for brands. What we come up with should deliver tangible results for our businesses, and forever wean us from our addiction to the imaginary benefits of branding.

Okay, there's one more important fact that I want you to remember: it's not just that branding doesn't work anymore, but that you can do something about it.

I don't presume to offer all of the answers to meet this challenge. But I'll be damned if we're going to continue avoiding the questions.

So good reading.

Better thinking.

And best *doing*.

Let's start throwing some wrenches into the gears.

CHAPTER 1

Your Branding Is Useless

I t didn't take me long to get sick of seeing the Burger King.

You know who I'm talking about. The mascot dude in the cape and crown, with that eerie plastic face frozen in a blank half-smile. He started being featured in commercials in 2004, and then appeared in a Halloween mask, NFL footage, a MySpace page, goofy homemade videos, faux TV news stories, and at least three video games.

No wonder I felt sometimes like he was stalking me. Lots of people felt that way and wrote about it on blogs. But this reaction, like the campaign itself, was celebrated in the marketing world as a brilliant branding exercise. The company's top branding guru explained that the company had *surrendered the brand to the "collective conversation."*[1] And it spent many, many millions of dollars to do it.

The only problem is that the King never sold a single hamburger.

You thought that maybe minds greater than yours had proof that such nonsense somehow made sense or that the branding didn't matter to you because you weren't the target consumer. Companies wouldn't do it otherwise. That's why branding is a fixture in our lives, much like gravity and taxes. It's been around since the Stone Age. Brands matter because, well, because they just do.

Nope.

The mascot didn't inspire you or anyone else to visit a Burger King per se. Most branding amounts to getting consumers' attention, and usually involves something funny, obnoxious, weird, stupid, overtly or implicitly sexual, or insanely abstract. A branding campaign is deemed a success if it gets people to look up from whatever it was they were doing, and then, when asked later on, admit that they remembered doing so. That's what mascots are all about. The rest of marketing is intended to get people to buy stuff. Branding *isn't supposed to sell anything more than an idea*.

Exactly *how*, *when*, or even *if* branding will influence consumer behavior are questions to which none of the rules of logic, financial reporting, or morality apply.

We assume branding has implicit, a priori value, like Platonic absolutes. Brands are so large and all-encompassing that they can be the cause—or excuse—for just about any communications activity.

So consumers shooting their own commercials and posting them on YouTube? *Branding*. Product references in news stories? *Branding*. Hosting a booth for folks to walk past at a trade show, or throwing a lavishly expensive party? *Branding*. Commercials that don't advertise a product feature or benefit? *Branding*. Magazine ads full of white space and small print? Well, you get the idea.

A TASTE OF REALITY

Remember Coke and Pepsi's dueling starlets back in the late 1990s? After more than a decade of battling for cola drinkers, both companies fielded teen pop stars in multimillion-dollar branding campaigns: Christina Aguilera for Coke, and Britney Spears for

Pepsi. The purpose was to associate each starlet's persona with her respective cola. Pepsi spent $8 million just to air Britney's commercials on the Super Bowl in early 2002. Christina's campaign ranged across commercials, the Internet, and many millions of in-store bottle and can labels. The media couldn't stop talking about how the two starlets were duking it out with one another, just like their corporate sponsors.

What did that branding accomplish? Well, it's hard to tell—which is common when it comes to assigning lasting value to brands (more on this in the next chapter). According to annual reports and media coverage, I can tell you that within the year, with its Pepsi brand sales stalled, Pepsi swapped Britney for Beyoncé. It chose to split its next Super Bowl expenditure among four different products. And Christina eventually ditched Coke, choosing instead to do international commercials for Pepsi.

But I'm sorry, I didn't let you respond: do you even remember these branding campaigns at all? If you don't, or do only vaguely, you're not alone. Few consumers cared at the time. The branding probably didn't sell six-packs at the food mart (the companies still had to run ads in supermarket circulars), make sales more likely (it's hard to believe that the endorsements drove people to their grocers), or directly produced profits for the businesses.

No consumer could have avoided all the noise about the singers, but I'd suspect the lasting impact was just about zero, by any meaningful financial measure.

A more recent example of this dichotomy between branding and business reality is Gap's participation in the (Product) Red campaign sponsorship, which in late 2006 was the start of a laudable five-year commitment to donate a share of profits to help eliminate AIDS in Africa.

Sponsorships and charity are two of the best ways to spend lots of branding dollars these days. Gap's execution of the campaign was totally sexy and right on, with good-looking stars and models wearing the stuff. Bono and Oprah kicked it off, which is sort of like having the endorsement of the pop culture Jesus and Paul. We're talking lots of publicity, and all of it the *right* sort. The purpose, look, and feel of the campaign probably mirrored the sensibilities of Gap's brand image.

Let me try some back-of-the-envelope math on what the branding delivered: according to publicly available info, I gather that Gap put an estimated $40 million into its 2006 holiday expenditure for the Red campaign, for which it promised 50 percent of profits to charity. Its fourth-quarter 2006 Red sales were approximately $103 million, so when you add the cost of merchandise, shipping, and store employee salaries, let's estimate conservatively that total costs were three-quarters of the sales. That left about $25 million, of which $12.5 million went to charity, leaving Gap with the honor of having spent five dollars for every dollar it collected for charity.[2] Perhaps not so coincidentally, by January 2007, on top of almost two years of flat or declining sales, Gap ousted its CEO, sort of put itself up for sale, and started slashing costs.

It defies logic that branding can succeed while a company fails, yet it is common doublethink in a vast majority of businesses today. Experts possess every rationale and tool to sense the presence of branding—focus groups, exit polls, follow-up customer surveys, even brain scans—all to explain that brands have value "out there" in the marketplace. When ad trade publications report on branding, it's like reading a movie review.

But there's no *there* out there.

I've spent my twenty-five-year professional career trying to understand why businesses tolerate this disconnect. I can't think of a type of branding exercise in which I've not participated, from old-fashioned PR stunts to newfangled viral campaigns. I've spoken on branding at top trade shows, written about it in academic articles, and covered it for years on my blog, Dim Bulb.[3] And after literally thousands of conversations with my peers around the world, I've got to come clean.

Branding is based on an outdated and invalid desire to manipulate and control consumers' unconscious. It looks good and feels good to the people who produce it, but it has little to no effect on consumer behavior. And if and when it does, there's no good way to know for sure. Companies do it mostly out of habit and hope, and most consumers endure it out of routine and indulgence.

Most branding is a waste of money.

Let's face it: Microsoft couldn't have expected to sell more software with its ads featuring dinosaur-headed execs a few years ago, could it? Citibank's egregiously artsy "live richly" billboards probably didn't prompt many new accounts, but was intended to somehow strengthen its image. And United Airlines' animated TV commercials and swooning soundtrack weren't supposed to fill seats on airplanes, necessarily, but to add to United's identity.

Right now, you can think of a business and recall a color, slogan, funny commercial, or other branding artifact. Yet will your thoughts survive until you get to the bottom of this page, or until the next time you get to a store? Are those thoughts impervious to the next blue screen of death, error on your bank statement, or canceled flight in your real life? Even if it has succeeded in capturing your attention and taken up residence in your subconscious, will branding influence your ultimate purchasing behavior? Are your memories formed in a way that reflects what the corporate sponsors wanted you to think? Do you maintain a *relationship* with brands? Can you even say that they matter to you at all, past your simple awareness and imperfect, impermanent recollection?

If only the answers to these questions were yes, but they're not:

- Sony can't charge more for a DVD player manufactured in the same third-party factory as its competition, yet its brand name is so loved and well-known that it's probably a proper name for babies in some countries.

- CareerBuilder.com could make all of us hoot and howl at its funny commercials, and spend many millions on Super Bowl ads with Internet tie-ins, but it likely still has to spend the same amount of money, time, and effort securing and keeping actual customers.

- There are few examples of "favorite branding" commercials, irrespective of how entertaining close-ups of a scantily clad model might be, that get anyone reliably closer to buying a Bud, Peugeot, or a bag of Pocky chocolates.

Consumers don't interact with brands. They buy **stuff**, and purchase **real things**.

The connections between brands and reality have never been more imprecise. Actually, for every vague case history that waxes poetic on the soaring brilliance of branding, there are many more specific, detailed examples of its irrelevance. In fact, most of the real-world results that are attributed to branding usually mask other drivers of business performance:

- Coke might publicly credit its brand, but what often drives quarterly sales could be as dull as a distribution deal in a far-away country.

- Nike's profits tumble (in part) because of the money it wastes on World Cup sponsorship, but it manages to meet sales goals in other, less glamorous ways.

- Verizon runs commercial after interminable commercial, but it spends a ton on making its call center service world-class.

Burger King's promotion of its creepy mascot covered up its abandonment of a health food menu, aggressive promotional pricing, and lots of other less sexy advertising that sold food to its customers. For that matter, McDonald's reported its best ever quarter during the same time period that Burger King celebrated its brand, yet it credited the very same dull, nonbranding activities that Burger King hid in its reporting.[4]

And Burger King isn't even one of the top twenty-five global brands, which annually spend in the tens of billions of dollars, pounds, yen, and other currencies on brand advertising. The amount spent on branding *overall* is many times more than that: we're talking about sums that top the GDP of most of the countries on the planet.[5] Forget all the real good that money could do, like eradicating malaria in Africa, or finding a cure for Alzheimer's. Think of the billions of hours of our lives wasted being subjected to the stuff.

Are you with me yet? *Branding just doesn't matter.* This is a big kahuna of a realization to get your head around. Kind of like all the East Germans waking up one morning and deciding that the Berlin Wall didn't exist anymore, and then, *poof,* it didn't. Or like telling your kids that there's no Santa Claus. You've still got to answer the question, *How the hell do you explain all those presents under the tree?*

To do so, you first have to make an important distinction: "Marketing" is anything that contributes to consumers buying something. It's the information that drives ads, product reviews in newspapers or online, and any of the other communications tactics that are intended to inform people of something that will (hopefully) move them to act.

"Branding" is the thinking that those tactics can do something more, something esoteric, like plant ideas or associations in people's subconscious that will, one day, influence them. It is the conceit that marketers can convince them of things that aren't substantiated by fact or the reality of experience, and that such inventions have an existence over time.

Branding is why so many of those ads, press releases, and other communications media we see either make no sense or, at best, make us briefly chuckle or gasp. Why slogans are incomprehensible, and comedic skits have no connection to what we might want to do with our money. It's why we get lifestyle ads that all look similar and why so many of those campaigns fail.

Branding is a hope wrapped in a desire inside a fantasy.

Now, imagine if you woke up this morning, and all of the branding in your life disappeared. No Burger King. No Geico cavemen, Churchill nodding dog George, or those cartoon characters hawking toe fungus ointment and sinus remedies. No funny beer commercials on TV, or logos on the T-shirts in your drawers. No "brought to you by" corporate names on stupid viral videos e-mailed to you at work, or plastered over your local stadium as you pass it on your commute. None of the noise that branding supposedly attaches to your life. Would you behave differently?

Nope.

You would continue to buy the best products and services for the money you're willing to spend. Companies would provide you with information, both factual and inspirational, which could be assessed depending on how close you were to making a decision. Your assessments would occur in real time, based on your interactions directly with companies, and your actual and virtual interactions with family and friends. You'd prioritize what you thought and bought within a *context* of time, place, mood, and price. By tomorrow, you'd shake it all up, depending on what happened during the day. Brands as shorthand? You wouldn't miss them, because today we take literal, verbatim notes—with pictures and sounds attached—and we do it 24/7. *Behavior*—buying something—is the only real evidence of your preference.

You wouldn't miss branding because you already live without it.

Consumers have access to too much information, face too many choices, and are too busy, impatient, and unforgiving. We don't internalize or use more than the slightest hint of all the words, images, sounds, and other contrived tools most branding utilizes. It's more *noise* than *context*.

And anyway, the idea that a marketer could fully analyze another person's thoughts and emotions has the romantic (and slightly scary) appeal of a Freudian fantasy, along with all the psychobabble mumbo-jumbo that comes with it. If we could get someone else to do things, everyone would be thin, nobody would believe in UFOs, and the Soviets would have won the Cold War. And our kids would do what we want them to do.

Some big brands, in fact, have actually disappeared one morning, after spending millions of dollars to establish all that equity in our consciousness: Cingular and Bank One both simply changed one day (to AT&T and Chase, respectively), as if a switch had been flipped, rendering all of the profound associations invested in those names either meaningless or, after many more millions, now somehow attached to newer brand names. The British post office spent £250,000 on branding experts to change its name to Consignia in 2001, and then spent another £1 million a year later to change it back.[6] Stay tuned for Christina to weigh in some time soon. For a price, of course.

The reality is that people purchase goods and services, not air. We've always bought *things*, not *ideas*. Sure, we *think* (at least most of us), but what is discernible, understandable, and measurable—to consumers, and within the businesses that sell to them—is what we *do*. We neglect Freud, and follow Skinner instead.

For every purchase, there's a *Donnie Darko*–like trail of events that led up to it, and another chronology extending into the future. Marketing works because it's the play-by-play for that behavior. Branding is nothing more than the color commentary, with the sound turned down most of the time.

So it just doesn't matter if gurus describe brands as stories, emotions, dreams, personalities, orgones, or waves of ESP. It's irrelevant, because it presumes to influence what people think. Branding doesn't do any of that anyway, or can only do it imprecisely and infrequently, if at all. Its real impact on how business is conducted can be seen in the contrasting examples of product development and positioning at Gillette and Starbucks.

When Gillette introduced its new Fusion, a five-bladed razor, there'd been no hue and cry from the marketplace about razors, no dissatisfaction with the shaves available from the already ludicrous (to some) less-bladed models. You can imagine the attributes that Gillette saw attached to the brand, and which they likely heard about when they asked consumers to think of things to say about shavers: *innovation, leadership, technology*. Assuming these vague perceptions were relevant, their belief drove them in the direction of developing a more complicated and expensive shaving solution. The magic of branding would enable the company's marketers to make consumers care about something they didn't ask for, don't need, and wouldn't want to pay for.[7] They'd buy instead the abstraction of the Gillette brand.

So far, the miracle of branding isn't working for them. Sales are lagging beyond expectations, though not for the lack of marketing expenditure, which started with a debut on the über-expensive Super Bowl in 2006. The branding consultants are advising patience, I'm sure, suggesting that it'll be years before the branding works. This would be in keeping with the Branding Guru Statute of Limitations (*you can't expect results until I've moved on to another branding job, or won a new client who can replace you when you fire me*). Gillette might succeed if it can simply stay the course, and in-store availability pushes out enough of the competition. But it remains to be seen whether it'll be able to do so with its predicted profit margins intact. Perhaps it can hope to win a branding award instead.

Starbucks is a different story. Many of us remember a cup of coffee as a fungible commodity, worth about 50 cents. It came in a waxy paper cup, sometimes coated with prints of faux Grecian urns. You bought it from just about anybody who was willing to sell it to you. Starbucks changed all that, "Holiday Inn-ovating" the tastes, cup sizes, store configurations, locations, and pricing, just as a new generation of consumers felt ever more chronically tired, and fashionably hesitant about appearing so.

It sure helps that its primary product is chemically addicting. But Starbucks is smart enough to recognize that its patrons don't consume image or any of the abstractions of brand associations. The Greek chorus of marketing media sings the praises of Starbucks as a brand, while its customers drink a potent brown liquid, and prefer comfortable and convenient places in which to purchase and consume it. So Starbucks focuses on making that reality better, faster, and easier. The few ads it runs—about bean farmers or the holidays—have so far remained a small expenditure, perhaps in passing deference to the output of Starbucks' consumer focus groups.

So call what Starbucks is doing branding, experience marketing—or call it *Fred*, for that matter. It *works*, because the company realizes that consumers no longer need (or want) the brand to mediate their experience. The conversation is not determined by the abstractions of color, imagery, or feeling, but rather the timing and the context of how consumers experience life.

How a company describes itself is a tactic. *The strategy of experience is branding.*

So, while Gillette wants to force consumers to behave in ways that coincide with its view of what the brand's feelings and emotions *should be*, Starbucks prompts behavior among consumers who have decided what the brand *is*. Brand *is* behavior, not something before, after, or apart from it.

Your own life experiences should confirm this fact. Have you recently tried to explain something to someone and had them either not understand a portion of it or doubt you entirely? How about making yourself known to someone who actively wants to believe you, like a spouse? Or what about having that understanding change, or fail to apply, when tested a moment, hour, day, or week later? Even on an interpersonal, one-to-one basis, and involving subjects that feature most prominently and matter most dearly in our lives—love and trust come to mind—we can't ensure that even the simplest thoughts will be shared, internalized, maintained, or used in the ways we intended for them.

Yet branding gurus think that they can make your thoughts and feelings about cheese spread or insurance far more explicit and dependable.

Our intuition tells us that if we tell someone something, they'll remember it. Yet most branding is delivered as if you met somebody who speaks a foreign language and, instead of translating the invitation to dinner, you grabbed their shoulders, shook them, and yelled loudly that they should be hungry. *Something* might get remembered, but it might not be what you intended, and it certainly might not prompt anything, or anything you'd wish to see happen.

Repetition is a fallacy, as anybody who sees the same commercial a second or third time in one sitting will tell you. The latest scientific research confirms this fact, yet it's still a standard branding practice. *Influence* is more of an ego trip than a strategy, since both science and business results confirm that people don't care much beyond their communities, virtual or real. In fact, branding doesn't sell anything other than the services of creative agencies, inches and bytes of media space, and a 767 to Google's founders.

Perhaps the scariest aspect of this reality is that *most marketers already know this.*

We've been talking about it for years, this disconnect between how people make decisions about products and services, and how communicators are equipped to communicate with them. You can't read a trade publication or attend an industry show without somebody addressing "the crisis in marketing," or "the challenge to traditional advertising." We've seen functional marketing—the stuff that should make somebody go buy something—get less effective, just as delivering it has gotten more expensive. People are harder to find, more difficult to convince, and less likely to remember what they're told. And I'm talking about giving them information they might *want* to know and use sometime. We need brands to do more, only we're getting less from them.

There's a multibillion-dollar Creative Media Industrial Complex dedicated to maintaining this status quo. It's an immense, well-funded, oftentimes brilliant edifice of proponents and beneficiaries dedicated to flushing money down the drain in perpetuation of a charade that hasn't been remotely relevant since the mass media days of the mid-twentieth century.

If branding is defined via ads and other media inventions, then there's serious money to be made inventing and placing it. There's a not-so-slight conflict of interest here, isn't there? Ad agencies are as much brokerage firms for selling ad space as they are stand-alone business propositions. Branding is the theology they perpetuate in order to sustain buyer demand.

Go to Amazon sometime and search for "branding," and you'll get a seemingly infinite list of *how-tos*, *then-fors*, and *what-ifs*. Most major universities offer advanced degrees, and produce a steady stream of scholarly thinking for other branding scholars' scholarly review. The Internet is chock-full of consulting firms offering branding principles, laws, rules, strategies, methodologies, and processes.

I can't help but think of the old aphorism: "When you own a hammer, all the world's problems look like nails."

Today, the vast majority of branding budgets are spent on campaigns that would be downright silly if they didn't cost so many companies so much money (and cost so many brand folks their jobs, as the chief marketing officer, or CMO, position in most companies offers the average tenure of a drummer for Spinal Tap).[8]

Although behavior is what marketers are actually *supposed* to care about—the whole point is to sell more, right?—the branding faithful have convinced businesses to spend money on something else, and then constantly struggle to convince consumers, clients, and bosses that they should ignore their senses (and good sense) and keep doing it.

The emperor always needs a new, very expensive suit.

Why do we keep buying it? The pundits will tell you that brands are a fact of life, emerging from a history that starts with symbolized hunting scenes of the Chauvet-Pont-d'Arc cave wall paintings 32,000 years ago.

Of course, it doesn't. Branding is not necessarily synonymous with handprints, symbols, labels, or regal crests. It's not the same as artists' signatures in the corners of paintings, political party icons, celestial patterns, or street signs.

We need to look past the shadows of our beliefs and expectations. What we'll see is about as meaningful as a Punch-and-Judy show, only we've been watching the shadows on a cave wall.

A *VERY* BRIEF HISTORY OF BRANDS

Subsistence economies marked experiential boundaries for most of the souls who've ever walked this earth. Generations of families lived and died on the same small, inconsequential plots of land, unless deprivation or hostility chased them to different, nearby inconsequential plots of land. There wasn't much choice in life, and purchasing or bartering was personal, regularly embedded in the knowledge and trust inherent in the tribe or community, and usually involved a specific, demonstrable value that the goods or services offered. You didn't trade for an *image* of something if it meant that you were going to starve.

A brand was the placement of a maker's mark on an object. It meant little more than asserting one's ownership, whether on roadside obelisks, porcelain, or cattle. What people *thought* or *felt* about the marks was usually irrelevant; the only impression that mattered was the visible indentation the hot iron made on a hide. That's why we don't find branding budget line items in the ledgers of Delft china makers, or image advertising expenses on the parchment of de' Medici business plans.

You'd have to squint through one eye to make the case for seeing branding anywhere in the world until the late 1800s. That's almost four thousand years after people first recorded doing business with one another.

The founding generation of America's branding gurus—people like J. Walter Thompson, Carl Byoir, Ivy Lee, James Ellsworth, and Bruce Barton—were born of a unique moment in time. Economies, society, and technology were undergoing massive change, bringing people together and enabling giant business conglomerates (just like today).

These pioneer branding guys worked for first-ever national companies, for which they created *corporate reputation* as a replacement for the reputations that individual businesspeople used to earn for themselves directly by their actions.[9] This is when we see companies first described as having *personalities* and *beliefs* via the new media of national news stories, ads, and, eventually, radio and TV.

But it certainly wasn't branding in any sense that we would use. It was too big, too diffuse. Ed Bernays, Sigmund Freud's nephew and another branding pioneer, helped increase cigarette sales for his Lucky Strike client in the early 1900s by inspiring *all* women to consider smoking, irrespective of product name.[10] He helped prove that the *collective id* could be manipulated using the limited media outlets that commanded attention and trust. But such manipulation could not necessarily be fine-tuned. This era of reputation work was all about changing basic behaviors on a society-wide basis, not necessarily (or only) establishing preference for one trademark over another.

A generation of advertisers around the world stepped up to do the selling work for individual clients: David Ogilvy, William Bernbach, and Marcel Bleustein-Blanchet advocated using the "new media" of the day for ads that sold benefits. They discovered that they could claim that a toothpaste would make you happy, or a washing machine improve the quality of your life, and a trusting audience of consumers, with limited access to dissenting points of view, would agree. Consumers believed what they were told, just as they had ever since the Ptolemites lectured them on complicated gears in the heavens. The ad people talked about brands, but they delivered marketing that sold stuff.

Madison Avenue then, like Silicon Valley today, stood for creativity, initiative, and success, and its output both drove and rode the wave of global post–World War II economic growth.

And it worked, because this first go-round with mass media marketing was truly able to sell on a mass scale.

Consumers were inspired to buy bigger and bigger cars. They shared experiences, important and inconsequential, like a giant, extended "global village" as envisioned by Marshall McLuhan. In this way, the Golden Era of Branding was a *command-and-control phenomenon*, no different at least structurally than the fascist and communist propaganda machines that had preceded it. There were no evildoers behind it, of course, but the mechanism and delivery were the same. And for about thirty years or so, the thoughts, feelings, and other associations of brands actually made a difference. Advertising delivered it, and consumers bought it.

By the 1960s, however, the Golden Era of Branding had already begun to show signs of wear.

The postwar boomer generation started to come of age, and with them came another epoch of dramatic cultural, technical, and social change. Individuals and society alike became more critical, self-conscious, and self-focused.

This made the declarations and contrivances of traditional branding seem unbelievable, disconnected, or irrelevant. So advertisers got more inventive and challenging, hoping to bridge that gap of perceptions: A distinction between *branding* and *marketing* was codified, and the distance between the two functions grew. *Branding* took charge of imagery, creative, and humor, all in the hope of overcoming consumers' growing mistrust, while *marketing* continued communicating product or service benefits.

For sure, sometimes the two intertwined and worked, such as when advertising innovator Stan Freberg broke lots of rules with campaigns like Contadina's "Who Puts Eight Great Tomatoes in That Little Bitty Can?" (1956). But his brilliance was far outweighed by a host of creative types who produced ever more abstract funny, scary, or simply incomprehensible advertising, all in service to brands over real benefits, and branding over sales.

So the promise of branding's miracle cures was too hard to forsake. Corporations remained addicted to the time-tested absolutes of brands as communications abstractions, only adding a new gear every time the last campaign didn't work. Principles and rules were drafted, academic programs founded, and a new generation of smart people assumed the mantle. Branding became something that companies *did,* separate from, or above, the rest of marketing.

Today, the spotlight of controlled media that once enabled companies to pretend there was a difference between the imagination of brand and the reality of marketing and business is no longer there. Any chance that branding can accomplish what we once hoped it would is altered through a mediascape that is:

- **Fractured.** The handful of networks available on broadcast TV have been replaced by a five-hundred-channel multiverse on cable and satellite boxes.

- **Diversified.** No two people watch the same shows anymore, nor does one channel (or medium) satisfy a single consumer's media needs.

- **Discredited.** The perceived veracity of journalism and commercial messages has declined, just as the amount of programming and number of voices have grown.

- **Replaced.** Video games, DVDs, DVR, and any number of other technologies and attitudes have not only dimmed the media spotlight, but often redirected it, or shut it off.

- **Repurposed.** Consumers no longer look to media to be informed, but rather as a process in which they participate and do the informing.

In fact, with the spotlight no longer in control, *people are going back to the future*, and participating in behaviors that would be very familiar to people who lived before the Golden Age of Branding.

Our "new media"—blogs, chat rooms, instant messaging, and virtual world communities—are celebrated by marketers as a brave new world for branding, but they're really *snazzy old ways*

of sharing and consuming. People have reverted to the same behaviors that have driven commerce since those cave walls were
first painted, relying on transparency, authenticity, interactivity,
virtuality, applicability, sustainability.

The brief twentieth-century interlude that was characterized
by top-down, authoritative mass media, and its trusty henchman
branding, is over. We still possess all of our hopes and desires, but
the world has changed.

We're back to painting the cave walls for one another, only with more money and better hygiene.

Brands are an artifact of a moment in time, a golden age when
they could be established, declared, delivered, and relied upon.
Branding now isn't something consumers want to "own," it's something from which they run or simply ignore.

Consumer behavior today is a far cry from what it was fifty
years ago. It's time to update our model and applications. This new
environment requires a new definition of brand.

WELCOME TO BRANDING ISLAND

Boss, boss, the brand, the brand!

Still wondering how we've got it so wrong?

You're not alone. Not only are many consumers very suspicious
of branding—assuming they don't ignore it altogether—but so too
are many businesspeople. By becoming a value that is intangible,
and therefore beyond the pale of all the other business practices,
branding is an activity that isn't held to the same standards as
the activities of the rest of the enterprise. This has kept both the
practice of branding and the structure and operation of marketing
departments stuck in the processes of the past.

Marketing is an island.

Trust your own experience. You've seen every other corporate department reborn over the past decade. Technology, management science, economics, and culture have caused gut-wrenching change in every area of the modern corporation, from individual job descriptions to the functions of entire departments. It might not be as exciting as silly homemade videos, but we're talking fireworks in the accounting or HR departments, which have redefined themselves to operate 180 degrees differently than they did even a few years ago. They're not just using new tools to do the same old things, but rather implementing totally redefined departmental purposes, reaches, integration, management, and measurement.

Conversely, marketing has remained an island. It's not enough to begrudgingly adopt a system to digitally store ad images, or some complicated "dashboard" with which to track expenditures. Since branding was first defined as nothing more than some sort of consumer awareness, marketing's strategic approach to it has remained mostly unchanged. The names and outlets are different, but the activities are more than a generation old:

- Instead of placing ads in *Look* magazine, we create buzz agent campaigns in nightclubs.
- Publicists no longer sell radio shows, they pitch bloggers instead.
- Whether distributed electronically or posted on an elevator landing wall, corporate communications departments are still focused on writing employee newsletters and quotes for press releases, just as they've done for generations.

Gregory Peck starred as a PR guy in *The Man in the Gray Flannel Suit* (1956). If he showed up for work today, he might not get some of the buzzwords or know how to send a text message, but he'd be otherwise very comfortable sitting in most any corporate marketing department or ad agency. The contrasts between the precepts of marketing and the changes that have washed over the rest of the corporation are quite striking:

- Branding still views consumers in terms of their supposed mental states, while the rest of the company sees behaviors.
- Marketers track feelings and other intangibles, while their brethren manage specific actions.
- Branding measurement is qualitative, while the rest of the company is quantitative.
- Marketing sees IT as a minor tactic, while the enterprise uses it as business strategy.
- The corporation changes and adapts in the face of change, while branding digs in to further justify the status quo.

And it's a wonder why CMOs get fired so quickly? Executive recruiter Spencer Stuart reported earlier this decade that the chief marketing officer job is one of the riskiest positions, with average tenure of 22.9 months compared to the 53.8 months for CEOs. The report cited *misaligned expectations* as the primary cause of this turnover. In my translation, that means brands deliver *awareness*, but the companies want to deliver *sales*.

Most marketers have yet to connect the dots on just how bad the problem really is. I know this amounts to heresy, but I offer you two facts:

1. Most branding doesn't do anything, so our definition of it as a communications construct is outdated, irrelevant, and costly.

2. Forget thinking about thinking; *behaviors*, not of brands but in life, are what matter.

The game has changed. You know it. So do the people around you, and so do the good folks who are competing with you. Circumstances have required the reinvention, recasting, outsourcing, or outright explosion of just about every single thing businesses do today. Except branding.

But maybe you still don't buy it. This book is going to work very, very hard to change your mind, because there is incredible opportunity ahead for businesses that embrace this thorny subject, and for individuals who choose to actively participate in finding new solutions. And there's great peril awaiting those who try to avoid it.

For branding to *mean* something, it has to *do* something, and I think it can. We can take it out of the realm of *thought* and connect it to *action*, relying not just on what it *says*, but rather on what it *does*. This would represent an enormous strategic and tactical change, on par with shelving Ptolemy's circles and gears, and replacing them with a more accurate, functional, and dependable model.

It means coming to terms with the idea that brand isn't a logo, ad, or creative invention. *Your entire business is the brand*, or, more specifically, *brand is behavior*. What matters is what you do, what your consumers do, and how all of those behaviors intersect with, influence, conflict with, and ultimately yield purchase behavior. As such, the responsibility to help deliver those purchases resides in every department (and with every external vendor and partner).

Brand is behavior.

So is distribution a brand strategy? Can sourcing be one? How about how people are hired, or how customer service is staffed and empowered? Merchandising decisions? What does customer relationship management, or CRM, do, or how will your telephone menus operate? The answer is *yes* to all of the above. Your entire company is in the branding business, for the brand resides in its real-time behaviors, not in its words or the colors used in its brochures.

When I was in college, my friends read *Rolling Stone*. I subscribed to *Advertising Age*. They worked at summer jobs waiting tables at seaside restaurants, while I trolled ad agencies to find work, drew layouts, and interned at PR firms.

So the subject of branding is a labor of love for me, and I know in the very fiber of my being that the relationship between consumers and products needs to be fundamentally redefined away from brand as a virtual construct of images and symbols. We need to conceive of brands instead as something more, something real, something that doesn't just suggest hoped-for thoughts and associations, something that doesn't presume to dictate to consumers what they should do, nor reduce information and icons to the raw materials for cutup videos and designs on T-shirts. Brand is behavior.

So start with this frightening thought: *your branding is useless*. There's no equity "out there." Nobody carries around in their heart of hearts little statues of what you've told them. Branding is a tax that your company pays for all the smart and creative people who could be delivering lots more value if they weren't wasting their time trying to hypnotize consumers.

Brand equity? Irrelevant. Brand identity? Who needs it? Brand strength? *It doesn't exist*. Skip your next branding strategy meeting, and read a few chapters of this book instead. It might save you a bundle of aggravation and money.

CHAPTER 2

Traces in a Cloud Chamber

About a hundred years ago, it was accepted wisdom that spirits exist.

The Society for Psychical Research, founded by scientists in the late 1800s, sent observers to séances and fact-checked instances of communion with departed souls. They compiled detailed notes describing revelations from the dead, such as learned secrets that had never before been shared, and remote transmission of conversations. The accounts were sprinkled with the occasional snare drum or trumpet suspended in midair, even a spectral appearance now and then. Many of the reported events delivered a sense of reality and meaning that defied explanation, as well as moved stoic disbelievers to tears.

Well, defied any explanation except for telepathy. *Mind-reading.* The society was convinced that some family members had skewed the results by sharing thoughts with the mediums.

They'd already documented hundreds of such cases. Telepathy was taken for granted: the remaining questions were simply to determine its qualities and limits, and how it colored conversations with spirits.

Imagine those scientists, dressed in their tweeds, hair parted down the middle and glued to their scalps, pencil nubs and worn notebooks in their hands, sitting ardently straight-faced as their subjects swooned and babbled in tongues. They *wanted* to prove their suspicions, but in the end their presumptions were based on too many beliefs that themselves required some good old-fashioned debunking. People had believed in spirits for centuries, so the researchers very well may have seen what they expected to see. But they were good enough scientists to admit, however begrudgingly, that it wasn't enough. They failed in their quest to objectively measure what was going on in people's minds, or what (or who) was communicating between them.

Measuring branding is in a similar predicament.

We certainly talk about brands like there's an *it* to talk about. Daily references in the news describe brands that can influence people and events at a distance, though brands also have characteristics that exist independently of both. Brands are a supernatural force, speaking through specially trained gurus who translate them for us in terms of perceptions, spirit, even soul. When researchers find proof, it's usually via modern-day séances, or *focus groups*. They expectantly ask subjects what they know about brands. The experts call this *aided awareness*. Videotaping is today's divining rod.

***

Brands are ghosts that everyone senses, but nobody sees.

***

To be sure, people don't need much prompting to recollect memories about brand names. You've likely bought a branded product or service since you started reading this book. Of course, brand influenced your decision: you were more familiar with one name versus another; your favorite brand offered a better value; perhaps a friend told you that it was a good deal, or maybe you can't really explain it entirely.

A brand is like a Platonic ideal, separate and apart from the who, what, where, when, and how of behavior. Brands just are.

But what is that influence, exactly? How did your knowledge of a brand affect your last purchase decision? How did it influence your subsequent purchase, or reflect your experience during the last? How did it come to be separate from what you learned and experienced for real, firsthand? Is there branding separate from behaviors?

There's no measure for any of this, other than lots of qualitative opinion and colorful analogy. You cannot effectively determine what influenced your decisions, and people are not reliable sources for assessing marketing's impact on themselves. In fact, brand marketers aren't good sources for clearly defined or reliable explanations, either.

It's stunningly odd that something so common in our language, and accepted in our reasoning, is so completely left outside of all the other definitions and measures businesses rely upon. Most companies know a great deal about impacts on profits and expenses. There are equations meant to calculate, and lines on balance sheets reserved to present, even the most infinitesimally small figures. Accounting is founded upon detail, and auditors earn their living making sure that every expenditure is represented and understood.

Every expenditure, that is, except branding, for which there is no consensus standard. Not even close. All we know for sure is that getting people to recognize a logo is usually a very expensive proposition.

Much progress has been made on analyzing return on investment, or ROI, for marketing activities, which we'll get to later in this chapter. But remember that marketing activities are distinct from branding:

- **Marketing** is intended to deliver actions, during a set period of time, with a cost and expected return that can be expressed on a spreadsheet.

- **Branding** is conceived as a far more subtle, intangible contributor to business performance. So, like stories scribbled during séances, it's instead perceived by any number of anecdotal measures.

MARVELOUS OBFUSCATION

To illustrate the predicament of measuring brand, let's look again at Coke, which is an easy target because it spends billions of dollars on its branding. Interbrand, one of the leading brand consultancies, declared that the Coke brand alone accounted for 51 percent of the stock valuation of the Coca-Cola Company in 2002. A few years later, a journalist explained the influence of Coke's brand had somehow transferred to the sensation of Coke's taste. Similar descriptions of brand importance and influence are quotable on any big company that spends large amounts of money on it.

Interbrand possesses a detailed methodology to substantiate its observations, however. In a selfless act of branding education, it partners with *BusinessWeek* every year to publish "The Top 100 Brands," touting an approach that "evaluates brands much the way analysts value other assets." Let's deconstruct it, and compile our own notes as the spirits materialize. The bold, bulleted points are steps in Interbrand's methodology:[1]

- **The projected profits are discounted to a present value, taking into account the likelihood that those earnings will actually materialize.**

    This starting point for the analysis is squishy, as the ability to assess the likelihood of any future event is inherently subjective. So the methodology will yield a *prediction* for the brand's *likelihood* of *contributing* to future earnings *potential*. The ranking is an estimate based on an estimate, two steps removed from objective measurement. We've already assigned a qualitative starting value estimate for what will include brand. And the calculating hasn't even started.

- **The first step is figuring out what percentage of a company's revenues can be credited to a brand (the brand may be almost the entire company, as with McDonald's Corp., or just a portion, as it is for Marlboro).**

  Wait a minute. Isn't this the entire purpose of the assessment? And consider the examples: Wouldn't you have guessed that McDonald's makes money from selling Happy Meals and that, if you could ignore nicotine's influence as a driver of consumption, Marlboro's revenues might conceivably come more from brand than the company? What's the difference between *brand* and *company*, anyway? Maybe the details of the methodology will clarify things.

- **Based on reports from analysts at J.P. Morgan Chase, Citigroup, and Morgan Stanley, Interbrand projects five years of earnings and sales for the brand.**

  Okay, more confusion. First off, financial houses have no standard analysis tool for assessing the value of brands. Most of them categorize brand as an *intangible*, and often don't dissect corporate marketing budgets with any distinction between brand versus marketing expense (machinations of *above* and *below* the line notwithstanding).

  When financial people use the word "intangible," it's code for "may or may not have any value." *Everything they care about is tangible*, and it all gets revealed on a spreadsheet. So Interbrand is taking financial firms' qualitative estimate of future performance, and building on top of it some guesstimate of branding's role? There's no real math here whatsoever.

- **It then deducts operating costs, taxes, and a charge for the capital employed to arrive at the intangible earnings.**

  Oops, maybe there is math after all. But what does it mean? The last step yielded earnings, which you get to only after deducting operating expenses and so on, but maybe they were talking about the business instead of the brand in the last step? And what is the expense for intangibles? Are expenditures for brand (exclusively) a cost item, or perhaps somehow considered an investment (brand equity) that's depreciated over time? The usage of capital is a fuzzy thing to estimate, at best.

- **The company strips out intangibles such as patents and management strength to assess what portion of those earnings can be attributed to the brand.**

  Stripping out lesser intangibles from the über-intangible of brand is a good thing, I guess, but it seems sort of random. How does Interbrand assign a number to *management strength* so then it can deduct it? Patents can actually be estimated, if only on the basis of the value of the legal rights themselves (let alone any market development), but how is it done here? Lots of qualitative opinion is getting passed off as quantitative measurement.

- **Finally, the brand's strength is assessed to determine the risk profile of those earnings forecasts.**

  Considerations include market leadership, stability, and global reach (or the ability to cross both geographic and cultural borders). That generates a discount rate, which is applied to brand earnings to get a net present value. *BusinessWeek* and Interbrand believe this figure comes closest to representing a brand's true economic worth.

Gesundheit! Just revel in all that broad, ill-defined double-speak: *risk profile, considerations, market leadership, stability, global reach, ability to cross cultural borders.* All these assessments and rates are qualitative estimates. This isn't math, it is religious scripture, created to reaffirm belief to the flock while ginning up enough obfuscation to dissuade nonbelievers.

Imagine if somebody else in your company tried to explain expenditures with the language of branding.

How about if the HR people talked that loosely about what they're doing? Or IT told the board that investments would yield *sorta-kinda-maybe-if-you-look-at-it-with-one-eye-closed* results? They'd get laughed at or fired, or both. The funny thing is that the Interbrand methodology for brands is one of the better ones. Consulting companies in every major market in the world happily spend client money on other methodologies to research brand among various stakeholder groups, and then portray it as a map, architecture, tree, or strand of DNA.

Just for giggles, ask someone who does branding for you to explain the process. If you do branding for your company or for clients, spend a few minutes analyzing how you go about validating your claims. Make note of every term or phrase that doesn't have a clear definition, and put an asterisk after every entry that represents a qualitative statement or judgment. Highlight entries that are declarative statements, such as "people will think this," or "be aware of that." Write an actual sales number at the bottom of the page. Then, when you're done talking with your expert (or being an expert yourself), take a breath, throw caution to the wind, and try to blow holes in the process. Take nothing for granted. When you hit the first term or step that doesn't have a clear purpose or connection to that sales number on the bottom of your page, look at the clock. My guesstimate is that it will take you under a minute to get there.

I can just imagine the collective *harrumph* I just got from any brand experts reading this book.

Actually, you can go to my website, baskinbrand.com, and post your opinions or complaints about this point (and any other in this book). I can predict that most of the posts on measurement will be numbers or ratios that have to do with awareness, impressions, or other intangibles. I considered hosting an X Prize–like competition to reward the first proof that brands exist, but too many people already believe they've proven it.

Branding serves primarily to perpetuate the belief in branding and thereby preserve branding budgets. I would be happy to be convinced that my thesis is invalid, but branding metrics today are circumstantial variables that yield fuzzy conclusions. Just like telepathy influenced studies of spiritual communication, marketers' beliefs in brands cloud their judgment on *what* and *how* branding might influence corporate performance.

Maybe brand experts are the wrong people to ask about measuring brands?

A VISIT TO THE DOCTOR

Magnetic resonance imaging research showed in early 2007 that neurons fire up more easily and happily at the mention of familiar brand names. Regions of the brain associated with more active cognitive work and negative connotations flame for weaker ones, which means people don't like having to work harder to recognize things.

These findings were like discovering wood chips from Noah's ark. The branding blogosphere went crazy with the wonderful news. The *Wall Street Journal* celebrated the breakthrough.[2]

The coverage was more subdued in its mention of two less thrilling findings: first, the research found *no connection whatsoever* between awareness and any subsequent action, and second, that there was no neural activity differentiation *between brands*. If the name was familiar, VU meters spun, whether for insurance or cars.

The research found proof of *awareness*, which is something anyone could have told them before they plugged the first test subject into a gizmo. Human beings have thoughts and feelings, and our brains are the places where ideas sizzle, crackle, and pop. The issue that remains unanswered for brand research is whether commercials, colors, and celebrity endorsements add up to something coherent, which then has a causal connection to subsequent purchase decisions.

There are connections between *thought* and *behavior*, of course. We don't operate on instinct alone, and our neural pathways aren't wholly predetermined by biology and chemistry. But trying to claim control of the former in order to influence the latter is the imprecise religion of branding. The connections aren't clear, dependable, or wholly real. And, so far, they're certainly not measurable.

Some scientific research offers very tantalizing and frustratingly incomplete hints of defining those connections, though.

In late 2004, researchers at Baylor College of Medicine found that test subjects preferred Pepsi in a *blind* taste test, but overwhelmingly chose Coke when the two cups were identified (their a priori expectations to choose Coke were determinant). The folks who selected Coke registered more activity in the area of the brain called the medial prefrontal cortex, which is associated with higher-level thinking. So their expectations about brand were preexisting, and served to overrule the feedback from their taste buds.[3] Another experiment reported by Boston College and Wharton evidenced proof of *conversational implicature* when consumers reacted more favorably to crazy, ill-defined names for crayons—razzmatazz, tropical rain forest—than they did to more descriptive labels.[4] It's as if our minds have parallel functions for predetermining reality, and actively construct it as we go along.

But these results are still a long way from measuring the true impact of brands. There's no causal measure for *what*, *how*, *when*, or *why* any preconceived notions about a brand got into the test subjects' brains, so it's unclear what, if any, impact branding activities had on those perceptions. Was NASCAR sponsorship important and, if so, more or less so than the memories of happy times in grade school drinking Coke with friends? How did the shape of the logo rank against the fact that one vending machine brand was consistently colder than the other? Did people like the color red over blue, or was it that Coke is reliably served at a favorite fast-food restaurant? Was price promotion at the local grocery a factor, and was it greater or lesser than the impact of a celebrity pop star endorsement?

Again, we don't need proof that people think things, or that our thoughts help shape our intended actions. The Greeks wrote plays about that.

If we're going to attribute the totality of all human existence to our theories about brands, well then, we're really in the realm of religious belief, not business or science. And we can endlessly study the physiology of brains and the influences thereupon, but it's a far cry from identifying which input triggers what output. Does branding prompt purchase? Does it support it, or make it more likely to repeat?

What we really need answered is the thorny challenge of measuring the existence and relevance of brands: *where's all the detail between awareness and eventual purchase behavior?*

We need fewer VU meters spinning, and more behavioral connections established between consumers and their choices.

There's a lot of science looking at how we make choices.

Researchers in Germany and the United Kingdom have used functional magnetic imaging to look at flashes in that medial pre-frontal cortex I mentioned earlier, and found a correlation between activity and subsequent action. They were able to predict with 70 percent accuracy if test subjects were going to do something they'd been asked to do.[5] Conversely, studies from Carnegie Mellon, Stanford, and MIT have illustrated that the immediacy of a purchase decision actually *deactivates* the medial prefrontal cortex, and suggests that emotions surrounding the perception of immediate benefits/trade-offs are what prompt decisions.[6]

So, in other words, science confirms that we human beings are just bad decision-makers. And branding doesn't make us any better at it.

I'm all for the discovery of a pill or an electric shock that will transform disinterested bystanders into engaged consumers, but it seems that we're seeing that the reality of consumer purchase behavior is constructed of two broad components: *context* and *experience*. Yet the Creative Media Industrial Complex goes on perpetuating the belief that companies should spend time and money not trying to influence what people *do*, but what they should *think*.

It's an alluring Freudian fantasy to believe that we carry embedded in us all of these subtle sensations about brands, but the science just isn't encouraging.

If you've ever bought an ad, or tried to find the benefit in publicity exposure, you've come across the "three times rule" that says, in various versions, people need to see something at least three times in order to remember it. This is often part of the argument for a minimum branding expenditure, which is usually more than what you want to spend.

It's also basically untrue: There's lots of research that says repetition not only doesn't increase retention, *but actually lessens it*. One study suggests that the first time something is repeated, there's a 42 percent decrease in mental activity.[7] You've experienced this phenomenon when your brain tunes out that regular, repeating drip from the kitchen sink, or when you see someone so often that you stop paying attention to what they're wearing.

You do the same to commercials on TV. Brand communications can work *less* effectively through repetition.

Some studies suggest that recognition will degrade less quickly if the initial message was meaningful or relevant to the recipient, or if it varies slightly each time it's presented.[8] So repetition works for actors and others who are doing something that they're already interested in remembering. But there's no concrete evidence that repetition improves anything for consumers past minimal name recall. It's just as likely to confuse.

Who cares if brain waves flutter but nobody buys?

There's some promising work under way to link awareness with behavioral action.

One research track claims to understand the sources for brand, and then allow for predictions of alternative brand-building strategies.[9] It models name/service awareness, attribute perceptions (like functions), and nonattribute perceptions (people's likes). When applied to a real-life case of digital cell phone competitors a few years ago, the model accurately mapped to real performance, allocating $127 million to a company as earnings from brand equity versus product and/or service value alone.

There remain nagging loopholes in the approach, however. Brand-building is a vague category of expenditures that focuses on communications, not business activities, such as changes in customer service or improvements in packaging. By categorizing its model as tracking *equity*, it lacks a dynamic link to situation and real-time circumstance, so its snapshots of what is or isn't brand may or may not be objectively valid. And there's no set period of time over which branding spending is tracked, so the model can't specify whether the return outweighs its cost. Perhaps most troubling is the fact that the strongest link is also the most broad and unactionable: the model proves that awareness has a generic benefit to sales. We already knew that.

It is every businessperson's dream to have customers arrive at the doorstep ready to buy. Better yet, people should arrive ready to be satisfied with their purchase. Branding promises to deliver this dream, and it's why any number of expenditures are tolerated. If brands could deliver familiarity, positive feelings, confidence, automatic credibility, the payoff would be huge. But it seems that the only thing branding delivers is *awareness*.

Marketers are talking to themselves when they qualify or parse what constitutes that awareness. Branding can help people recognize a name or logo; there's no disputing that fact, and you can imagine the simple equation that greater awareness means a larger pool of potential consumers, which in turn should translate into greater sales. But awareness isn't set in stone, *it's a moment in time*. There's no way to ensure that things are attached to it, whether you hope they're perceptions, nonattribute associations, or colors of the rainbow.

There's no *it* that exists independent of each individual experience, nor separate from any moment in which *it* is pondered or reported. And that dream about customers arriving at your doorstep already presold on buying from you? It's just a dream, and you know it.

We carry with us beliefs and expectations that affect our choices, and influence our experiences of them.

Our beliefs and expectations are a list that is constantly updated, both consciously and unconsciously. We reorder it based on mood, circumstance, and opportunity. It's a wholly subjective and fluid feedback loop. It's also a filter. Our past experiences affect what we choose to contemplate, how we consider it, and our conclusions derived thereupon. Nothing is concrete or unchanging. Our brains are marvelous machines that quite literally re-create reality moment to moment.

Awareness is but the start of a long process, full of variables, influences, and decisions through which your customers must travel. Very little of what happens along the way has anything to do with branding as currently practiced. So if researchers discover the seat of brand in the human soul in the next few years, it'll certainly have implications far beyond marketing strategy. But we can leave that to the purview of other publishers and pulpits.

Let's talk about how we plan brands based on what we know about the reality of behavior.

A VERY LONG CORRIDOR

People who sell for a living see a *leaky sales funnel*, or a winnowing process that starts with lots of potential at one end, and ends up with only a portion of that opportunity realized at the other. The visualization is usually shown vertically, to suggest some natural movement from the top down. I've used a version of the funnel to visualize behaviors with my clients, only flipped it on its side, so the movement is *across* the page.

Broadly speaking, the funnel metaphor organizes the steps—each a collection of moments that have rational and emotional dimensions—that will move a consumer from awareness, to purchase, and then to repeat purchase. Our funnel divides into five major categories:

1. **Problem recognition**—Perceiving a need
2. **Information search**—Seeking value

3. **Evaluation of alternatives**—Assessing value

4. **Purchase decision**—Buying value

5. **Post-purchase behavior**—Value in consumption or use

There is an order to the steps, a *Chronology of Purchase Intent*, with little latitude of movement between steps. A message to trigger purchase decision (4) falls on deaf ears if someone is simply searching for information (2). Conversely, providing general background information (2) is useless to someone who is ready to decide (4), or is already consuming the product or service (5). Each step is dependent on all that go before. It is a continuum, or a continuous endless succession of hallways through which your customers must walk. And those hallways evolve in shape, texture, and content as consumers travel through them.

So imagine that you're not happy with your toaster. It toasts unevenly, or you can't fit bagels in it, or whatever. Maybe you do some homework on toasters, whether online via search or standing at the store shelf and reading display signs. Perhaps you ask a friend. Or maybe your toaster no longer works and you just need a replacement. Perhaps you want a certain color, size, timer, and so on. These are discrete steps in a journey you take—from old toaster to new toaster—and this journey is driven by your needs, your desires, your timetable, and whatever else you choose to care about.

Now, think of how traditional branding applies to this (your) Chronology of Purchase Intent. How many times have you seen an ad, or had a store person tell you something, and had absolutely no idea what it meant? Or why it was relevant? Forget all the jokes or oddity that marketers use to try to catch our attention. I'm talking about examples where branding was just nonsense.

How about learning something about a brand that prompted more questions you couldn't get answered? Consider the proliferation of icons and logos that appear on every product, staying true to the brand but explaining nothing to you. Ever see a special price on something, but you weren't able to figure out if it's a good deal or not? I know I have.

In a world where we're constantly faced with new, nearly ubiquitous access to information—and marketers have nearly equal access to us, via the various new gizmos we enjoy—the sales funnel/hallway starts to look like a crazy, mixed-up hall of mirrors, instead of a thoughtful pathway.

That's because traditional branding treats those points in the funnel as *mind states*. Awareness is an absolute, and branding is decided on what consumers should know and feel. Branding is created to try and manipulate what you think about brands, not how brands (or the underlying products and services) relate to you. It's left up to the consumer to find relevance in brands, instead of the other way around.

So addressing the steps in the actual Chronology of Purchase Intent usually defaults to the salespeople to make it work, usually with price (since that's all they have to work with). The steps in the eyes of brand folks mostly default to fate and chance. Brands are propagated into the universe and, hopefully, something will trigger their applicability to your life.

Maybe you're doing it right now: running marketing that purports to expose your consumers to your brand, with the vague expectation that it'll do something, somehow, some time later on.

But take awareness off the table for a minute. How does any of the branding you produce apply to steps in the chronology of your consumers' journey to, and through, purchase?

**Chances are that your consumers' journey
is left to chance.**

This is why we might want to reconsider the parameters of the measurement challenge itself. What if:

- Brand were defined as *what your consumers do*, and
- Branding defined the *who, where, when, why,* and *how* that delivers it?

Awareness could be a *factor* in that equation, but only the start. We'll explore this approach in detail through the book, but now is a good time to start toying with it.

Here's a hypothetical example: Travelers, which in 2007 bought its trademark red umbrella from Citi, then rolled out a branding campaign based primarily on awareness and recognition of that icon. Its ads effectively announced, "Think of us, because we've just invested a lot of money in buying this logo." It was really an extension of its recent esoteric branding TV campaign, which featured a giant ball rolling downhill and destroying everything. Back then, the punch line was "When you have insurance that stays in sync, you can roll with anything." Ad industry sages gave it glowing, five-star reviews, noting its deft expression of the human comedy. It was clearly a brilliant effort to get recognition, while declaring associative benefits for the Travelers brand.

Got it. If I were paying exclusive attention when this aired, and at that very moment contemplating insurance, I just might have given Travelers a shot, although not necessarily. I could have otherwise ignored or forgotten it. Or simply not understood its art.

Like seeing a corporate logo on a billboard at a baseball game, there was no strategy to attach the branding to my behavior.

What might a behavior-based, chronologically sensitive funnel have looked like for them:

- **Problem recognition.** Most of us don't think about insurance unless a crisis occurs, which is obviously too late. So why not identify moments when crises *are about to occur,* or could happen? Wouldn't ads on the Weather Channel make sense? How about sponsoring storm coverage? If Travelers targeted events rather than user demographics, it might yield an entirely different media buy. Start feeding the funnel here.

- **Information search.** Again, most of us are either under- or overinsured, but we have no methodology for knowing or resolving it. Could Travelers register people for free, or provide immediate assessments of coverage, much like the rate referrers already do online? Why not create a knowledge program that locks people in years before they need or change insurance, and use that time to educate them while giving them some beneficial uses for that knowledge? Don't tell me about the brand, because at this point I don't know what I don't know.

- **Evaluation of alternatives.** Isn't all insurance generic in the end? If not, there must be actions that differentiate Travelers products and services. A snowball is certainly not one of them, nor is any appearance of the red umbrella icon. Couldn't there be events built around these points of difference? A better risk assessment tool, perhaps? How about campaigns to help people assess competitive policies they may already possess?

- **Purchase decision.** There must be ways Travelers could make a purchase decision easier, or a more compelling value. Software and Popsicle companies alike use *sampling* as such a tool. So does Apple in all of its retail stores. How about some entry-level coverage deals? Or how about linking the cost of transferring a policy to an impending crisis, like offering a discount on tornado coverage on websites when a funnel cloud is so many miles away?

- **Post-purchase behavior.** I have to imagine that customer service is the toughest part of providing insurance, in that it's in Travelers' best interests to minimize payouts (just like health care). So could Travelers invent events for post-purchase support that are a true value-add? How about pre-crisis coverage alerts, or post-event co-selling linkups to service providers that help fix roofs? Help reduce the need for payouts and strengthen consumer loyalty at the same time.

These aren't intended to be actual recommendations, but to illustrate a point: The big idea about the brand would *not* be a giant snowball rolling through an effects-laden TV commercial. It wouldn't necessarily come from marketing at all. Instead, the branding campaign could focus on the equation consumers go through to examine, purchase, and keep insurance policies. It could offer any number of points at which would-be consumers could start a direct dialogue with the company.

Behaviors along the Chronology of Purchase Intent become the brand.

Now, the gurus really don't care about understanding such an equation, because its variables of time and space are beneath the more profound domains of consumer thought and feeling. Branding presumes that it can create and adjust ideas. There's a vast array of mumbo-jumbo words and terms to substantiate such claims of influence.

But imagine each element of your branding prompting a behavior, then leading to a follow-on event that you also can hope to help prompt and build upon. Some dependencies emerge quite naturally from this sort of approach. It would be obvious that before someone could do B, they had to know and do A. Or that it's pointless to tell them X when they're doing Y, no matter how funny the agency makes it.

Others points would require a lot of creativity. The result would be mappable and measurable, and the opportunity would be to formalize those events into a behavioral map that goes far beyond the Travelers example. You could strategically define your branding, or relationship planning, with your targets in terms of behaviors:

- **Who** your targets are
- *What* you want them to do
- **Where** you expect them to do things
- **When** you think things happen
- **Why** the current step will lead to the next one
- **How** the steps will link into an expression of brand

Conversely, most companies approach branding like infantry troops in a trench faced machine guns during World War I: *Heads up, boys, we're going over the top again!* It's almost the definition of clinical insanity when you expect a different outcome from doing the same thing over and over again. It doesn't help that any variety of self-anointed expert is happy to prescribe a treatment for the problems facing branding, or that different corporate departments are suffering from the lack of a common definition and solution.

So as every day passes, the system chugs on, spending money, describing its actions in glowing slide presentations, and having vague, if any, positive impact on your business. You can probably name a nonsense branding activity that's in your company's plan sometime soon.

Chances are it's going to fail. Worse, there'll be no good way to know if it succeeds. I'd put money on the only dependable result being that you'll be advised to do *more* of it.

Hey, that's the ghost of my cow!

The news on the measurement front is not terribly exciting if you want to find hints of the existence and relevance of brands. It's no different than staring at a mirror in a darkened room and realizing that the gauzy spirit staring back at you is really your own reflection:

- **Marketers have no reliable measure for brands,** because we choose to define them in ways that are simply unmeasurable.

- **Science doesn't either,** whether trying to prove the presence of brand information, or find any connection to subsequent behavior.

- Thus, all we can say for sure is that **branding might help create awareness,** and that awareness is generally better than nonawareness.

Awareness is the first step in any sales equation, whether viewed as a funnel, long corridor, or row of spinning plates on sticks. By any measure, it's still a step that arguably has no inherent value alone, although branding gurus would want you to believe otherwise. Some companies have methodologies (or egos) that argue for awareness as some absolute. They leave it to the rest of the business, or to chance, to figure out how to measure its connection to marketing.

My curiosity about this conundrum took me to Seattle, to attend a training session on marketing return on investment (ROI) hosted by Jim Lenskold, a former AT&T exec and author of the definitive book on the subject, *Marketing ROI: The Path to Campaign, Customer, and Corporate Profitability.*[10]

Jim maintains that approaches to brand don't suffer a measurement issue, but rather one of strategy, in that many marketers lack clarity on what outcomes they expect, at what time, and how that ultimately influences short-term or long-term contribution to sales. Those companies that have a vision for how their brand marketing will influence purchase decisions usually can put reliable measurements in place, and deliver on objectives.

In this sense, *he treats branding as part of marketing*, which means it involves behaviors and is measurable. When the brand goal is longer term, it simply requires building connections between perceptual impacts and future behaviors. There's a lot more to measuring marketing than tracking responses to an ad, and I think Jim is very wise on the subject. I asked him to elaborate on the challenge of measurement.

"There are three ways that brand marketing can contribute to achieving business growth, in addition to the impact on stock price and price premiums," he replied. "First, it can increase early stages of the customer buying cycle, such as awareness; second, it can influence customers in all stages of the buying cycle, generating incremental sales by increasing overall effectiveness; and third, it can help shift long-term competitive positioning by reinforcing key functional and emotional attributes, thereby impacting future sales.

"With the right measurement methodologies in place, we can answer questions, such as, 'What does our brand marketing add to the overall marketing mix?' and 'What is the incremental contribution?'" he continued. "As we effectively shift our competitive position, or engage customers, or build the belief that there is a personal fit with our brand, we can detect the impact on behaviors, and the value that contributes.

"One of the key drivers of ROI is the customer value, which is very often more dependent on the repeat purchases than the initial purchase. So the brand marketing can bring a customer in the door, but the brand experience has much greater weight in the financial returns from that marketing."

So think about it, I say, maybe next time you're faced with the opportunity to choose between running an ad somewhere with your company logo on it, and putting the same amount of money into improved customer support for a few days. Maybe it's not worth it to try to "find" brands anymore at all, but instead to focus on what you do, what your customers do, and how it integrates into experience pre-, during, and post-sale. Think behavior instead of awareness, and you'll find a lot more to measure. In doing so, you might rediscover your brand after all.

Jim added a thought: "The discipline of running ROI analyses to quantify the assumptions of the expected impact from our marketing investments forces marketers to think about the touchpoints that follow, and the stages necessary to convert impressions to sales. With even basic steps to improve measurements of the return of specific marketing activities, you'll start making better, more effective and efficient decisions."

Wait! In the cloudy mist . . . *I can see it!*

CHAPTER 3

The New Nike

I was late as I walked to my office, so I almost didn't answer my mobile phone.

"I'm not going, just so you know," an associate declared. He was supposed to be on a plane to New York for a meeting later that day. It was September 11, 2001.

When I got to my office and figured out what was going on a few minutes later, I immediately called my wife, and then my daughter, to make sure they were safe. We were eight hundred miles away from New York, but that didn't matter. Reaching out to family and friends is a common, almost reflexive reaction to this sort of prompt. As such, there's much we can learn from it.

Guerrilla marketing got big in the 1980s as a way to market and brand on a shoestring, usually via unconventional ways that often meant that consumers didn't know they were being marketed to. It was so catchy and successful that its tools have become standard, very unguerrilla-like corporate operating procedure.

There's new guerrilla marketing being conceived today that gets people to react, to respond, and to ultimately change their behavior. And it's not best exemplified by supposed "guerrilla" marketers. Getting me to make that phone call to my family illustrated the potential for one of the new tactics for branding coming from today's headlines.

Terrorism as a branding strategy? I know, nuts, right? But please, bear with me.

What they say and do, and how people react, is a complex web of actions, upon which a lot of thoughtful books and commentary have been written. You could argue that terrorism is a tactic to promote a political or religious strategy goal, or that democracy is a political philosophy for which life, liberty, and the pursuit of happiness are enabling tactics.

I want to forget the politics and talk about how they're so successful at spreading their branding.

It's a pretty strange situation, if you think about it. Traditional marketing draws on the expertise that convinced the world to smoke Lucky Strikes, fly Virgin, drink Coke, shop at Tesco, wear Target, watch EuroSport, play on Sony PlayStations, and eat at McDonald's.

Today's bad guys offer nothing as immediately easy or attractive, and have no repository of branding skill upon which to draw. They're hawking burkas, beheadings, and the other benefits of living in the fourteenth century, *and yet they are successful*. Guerrilla marketing has broken every rule in the standard corporate marketing best-practices playbook. And if you think their branding strategy is as simple as wreaking havoc in front of TV cameras, you're missing the point.

Guerrilla marketers break the rules of guerrilla marketing.

Like any situation or circumstance, the environment and the rules have evolved. What was once guerrilla is now status quo, and the norm of many branding campaigns is the failure to trigger any measurable response beyond bland awareness. Today's terrorists are selling the corollary of curdled milk, or electronic gizmos that won't work. *Yet you can't avoid responding to it.*

Nike built its brand on many of the truisms of classical guerrilla marketing. As the corporate world has copied and adopted many of those techniques, the real guerrillas have leapt ahead with new tools, bringing new dimensions to their efforts. Not surprisingly, those dimensions are all about getting people to do things. It's branding conceived as behaviors.

So maybe we can learn something about guerrilla marketing by studying the guerrillas.

AN *IT* TO DO

Think of the last time that a business strategy in your company called for educating consumers to do things differently. Internally, there's likely been a *change management program* under way some time over the past few years, usually intended to teach employees how to use a computer system that replaced inefficient activities— you know, like banishing note-taking with pen and paper—with an enterprise-wide integrated electronic knowledge management data capture system (with extra stalagmites or something).

Contrary to the optimism of most branding gurus, ask any educator, and they'll tell you that the way human beings learn is by taking small steps that build on steps already known and practiced. And as any historian will confirm, we're doomed to repeat the mistakes of the past. People simply rename actions they already possessed and planned (i.e., do what they were already going to do). Habit is one of the strongest, most intractable qualities of life. On the spectrum of intensity of conviction, *habit* is to the left of *addiction*. *Routine* is just to the left of that.

Today's guerilla branding builds on people's fears of the unknown, just as it feeds the ignorance and anger of its proponents. It's as close to being *automatic* as branding can get. It triggers thoughts and feelings that are familiar, so it's really just a label, or an aggregator of known concepts. I get the brand pretty much out of the box.

That's why Nike is celebrated as one of the original and most effective guerrilla marketers. We can get distracted by the swoosh logo and the activists who protest the ubiquity of its logo, but the strength of Nike's branding is that it gave people a way to act upon desires that they already possessed. "Just Do It" wasn't a branding campaign to teach anybody anything; it simply stated what they already wanted. It doesn't really matter if you actually become a jogger, or if the shoes you bought ever touch a running track. Nike required you to do nothing new, and thus think nothing different. It exists in backhand deference to your inaction.

Your habits are your habits, and they likely include a latent desire to be more active. So, ultimately, "Just Do It" meant "buy Nike shoes," or clothes, or sports equipment. If you actually used them, all the better, because you could buy more. Nike has never tried to change what people think, but rather to attach a behavior to what they already believed. Thirty years and billions of dollars in sales later, Americans are more obese and sedentary than ever before. So *they're not doing it*. Nike has changed nothing, other than enriched itself beyond measure by selling its products, which in business is a very good thing.

It's the same general backstory for most successful branding in recent memory, although you'd never hear it expressed as such.

Riding waves works far more sense than creating them.

A few years ago, the tourism authority for Las Vegas started telling people, "What Happens in Vegas, Stays in Vegas," almost daring them to indulge in whatever personal definition they might have of doing something better left undisclosed. Who cares what they might do? The Vegas branding wasn't about teaching anything, but rather enabling potential visitors to label their own personal expectations. It allowed every adult to consider him- or herself a potential troublemaker, whether or not they'd actually make good (or bad) on it. Being ever so slightly bad is probably a latent desire almost as profound as our need to lose weight.

Contrast that with any of the tourism campaigns that invite people to "explore" or "experience" someplaceoranother, accompanied by beautiful, vaguely inert shots of beaches, ruins, and happy families. We all like the idea of a pretty seashore, *but so what*? Vegas stands out because it's all about *behavior*, not presenting a static concept of *destination*. It provides a reason for traveling. *Just do it*.

Subway is another example. So much of the fast-food business is based on habit and circumstance. There are definitely the die-hards who will never bite into one hamburger over another, but most purchase decisions are made based on routine, or on whether there's a clean, accessible outlet nearby when hunger pangs strike. That's why you see most of these companies play to type in their marketing.

Being *the best food that's bad for you* is what drives purchase, when trying to offer bad food that's good for you usually doesn't. It's why so much money gets poured into store renewal and upkeep. It's also why so much of the lifestyle branding around these businesses simply makes no sense, and offers such a contrast to Subway.

By marketing itself as the effective *healthy alternative*, Subway recognizes the importance of habit, and the likelihood that people will, at some point, some time soon, want to grab fast food. I don't think they expect anybody to go out in search of Subway because it's good for them, because it isn't. *It's less bad*. Subway isn't a lifestyle or a destination, but simply an alternative choice. Subway's branding focuses on that moment-of-purchase decision. Try to compare each penny spent doing that with the many, many pennies Burger King spent getting us to remember its creepy mascot.

Or think of how many products offer "enhanced" or "improved" functionality. Each is tacit acknowledgment that the easiest way to engage consumers is to give them more of what they already know and do. Experts view this as extensions of brand, when it's really *adaptations of behavior*. The latter approach leads to lots of costly, failed new product launches, in instances when the *idea* of the improvement doesn't fit the *reality* of prior behavior.

It happens a lot in the high-tech gizmo category, when a technology toy is an improvement that's obvious to the brand*ers*, but isn't so obvious to the brand*ees*. Can you explain the differences between your current and former versions of computer virus protection software? Are you one of the majority of people who uses about 5 percent of the functions on your mobile phone? Did you run out to buy all that extra functionality in Microsoft's Vista operating system, or are you still trying to figure out how to program your VCR?

Guerrilla branding gives consumers lots more for little to no extra effort.

I'll certainly pay a little more if my toothpaste will also improve my memory, or tie my shoes, as long as I don't have to brush differently. Similarly, successful guerrilla marketing tracks with known behaviors, and builds upon them.

A few years ago, I was involved in designing a corporate intranet for a financial services client. The internal system promised to give employees everything they'd ever need, all in one resource: directory, policies, forms, company library, travel services, you name it. Our biggest problem was that employee usage of such sites was dicey. It represented a gigantic change in behavior, all in the spirit of improvements to efficiency and efficacy.

When we studied employee behaviors, we learned that they all did something, and did so almost simultaneously: They checked the day's cafeteria menu, which appeared on flyers posted in every elevator lobby. So we configured the intranet to make this notice dominate the daily welcome screen, which also forced us to prioritize the other notices presented to employees. We had almost 100 percent usage on day one, and it stayed good, even if we risked branding it as a glorified restaurant menu. *We'd branded a new product based on actual behavior*, not hoped-for intent. No brand attributes. No psychological nonsense. It was pretty obvious that employees were hungry and curious, and upon that behavior we built brand loyalty to *using* the tool, not being aware of it.

SHUT UP AND SELL TO ME

How often have you heard about the crucial importance of *brand integrity*, or seen significant time and resources expended on making sure that your branding is applied across your business? Many books and endless consultants study and recommend branding as the "look and feel" of what you present to the outside world, the presumption being that it's important that everybody get the same information on your brand.

Yet we know from science and our own experience that information doesn't get transmitted like that at all. It's a bane for artists whose creations are intended to *say* one thing, but people internalize quite differently. One person's happy song is another's sardonic complaint. A painting can appear true to life or as a layered distraction, depending on the viewer.

The same thing happens in business. Internal communications again is an easy example: companies often try to label behaviors with explanations that fit the corporate liturgy, or dictate to employees how they should react to news. You can count on one hand the number of employees who believe pronouncements from corporate communications departments, unless you categorize the many flavors of *distrust* as a single reaction. I bet your company's PR department has labored far more over the wording of a particular sentence in an announcement—perhaps making a vague or strained interpretive point about something, usually bad news—while thinking far less about how employees will actually *react*. There's usually no plan to address those likely reactions, except with more pronouncements and other communications.

Communicators think they own ideas, but actually words and images are translated into behaviors that are owned solely by the recipients. It's why every invented reference to layoffs as "right-sizings" or "strategic reductions" usually not only fails, but hurts employee morale.

Guerrilla marketers don't tell, they show.

We did an experiment on this point years ago when I ran employee communications at Blockbuster. It was 1997, and the company had just relocated to Dallas from Fort Lauderdale, leaving lots of employees behind. Those who'd made the move were understandably suspicious of executive intentions, and a bevy of new staffers really didn't know what to think. The idea of issuing a company newsletter full of corporate declarations about the company just didn't feel right to us. So we hatched a different idea: We gave up ownership of the regular employee communications vehicle to a member of my team, whose job would be to distill corporate news and present it to employees.

She was an *anticipatory ombudsman* with complete independence, allowed to interpret, react to, and challenge news and, in doing so, anticipate employee reaction and behavior. Every news item had a next step (vote, comment, etc.). Bad news was reported as such, without spin or throwaway defenses. Good news was celebrated. She called the communication "Trash" (though HR didn't like it, so we changed it to "You Name It"), and its production value was distinctly low-res. The piece received incredible support from the employees. Our behavior allowed them to behave in ways they found most natural and genuine.

Nike's early days are a great example of the externalization of this approach. Founders Phil Knight and Bill Bowerman, runner and coach respectively, initially resold to actual competitive runners the shoes they distributed for a Japanese manufacturer. The Cortez, Waffle Trainer, Tailwind, and other early shoe designs were used by people to train and play sports. There was no celebrity endorsement strategy, nor some idea of associating with athlete name recognition, because many of the athletes early on had no name recognition whatsoever. *They simply used the products.* The activity was genuine, and it formed the foundation for everything that followed, from product development to marketing.

Nike's branding allowed consumers to associate their behaviors (contemplated or actual) with purchasing and using the products. Billie Jean King, John McEnroe, Michael Jordan, and Tiger Woods all followed this model. Their primary value was and is demonstrating *authenticity* to consumers. Like the newsletter at Blockbuster, their behavior told people, *I use this, so it's okay to buy it.*

Today's guerrilla branding isn't about getting consumers to think about celebrities any longer, or to somehow absorb images or associative feelings from them, necessarily. Rather, it's about giving consumers the reason and confidence to *act*, and the best way of doing do is by showing them behavior that they can understand and trust. It's all about *doing* things, not about *saying* things.

Of course, we marketers don't see it this way. We tend to elevate this simple behavioral fact into esoterics of image and emotional associations. If the terms of the deal are to get quick recognition and passing awareness, endorsements are an easy, though expensive, way to achieve both. If all branding is supposed to do is start the sales funnel we talked about in the last chapter, it makes complete sense.

Think of the billions of dollars wasted on endorsements, and all of the convoluted thinking required to legitimize it.

Celebrity endorsements confuse expectations for what consumers will *do* with what they *see*.

How many times can you remember a celebrity, but not recall the product for which he or she was shilling? Or consider the moment when Michael Jordan went from educated user to dabbling creator, *and was asked to design shoes*. One could start tracking the possible degradation of Nike's branding from *authentic design* to *fashion statement* with this moment. The number of celebrities who have sold their names to perfumes, or let studio engineers create albums for them, further highlights this once-valid strategy gone haywire.

One of its most egregious examples was when, in late 2006, Budweiser invited rapper Jay-Z to not only appear in commercials but to attend marketing strategy meetings. Talk about the ultimate awards show goodie bag! Paying celebrities for jobs they aren't qualified to do would be a questionable practice, if it were ever held up to real business scrutiny.

Paul Coletta, JambaJuice's CMO, has responsibilities far beyond marketing, including product innovation and store design. This brings many elements of brand behaviors under his purview, so it's not surprising that he has a very different, cutting-edge guerrilla vision of sponsorships.

"The traditional sports marketing model is broken," he explained to me over dinner in San Francisco. "There is little value in associating brands with athletes who can be bought by the highest bidder, or having products juxtaposed with their performance and hoping there's any lasting associative benefit in the minds of consumers. Most sponsorships and celebrity endorsements face the same difficulty. Just think about the NASCAR cars and drivers covered with logos. It's nothing better than brand soup.

"Jamba has a different approach, which evolved out of a philosophy developed with consultant Ken Sacher, which we call 'Patriots and Mercenaries.' Mercenaries go to battle with no interest in its outcome. They fight because they're getting paid, and they'll collect whether the battle goes north or south. Patriots do battle because they want to win. Their hearts are in the game, and they share in the success or failure of the endeavor.

"Consumers see the difference, and they know it instinctively. That's why we want patriots as partners, and we've applied it as the guide for selecting our sports marketing ambassadors as follows:

- Jamba Ambassadors are authentic. They love our product, believe in our mission (to inspire and simplify healthy living), and have a relationship with our team members.
- They pay exclusively for Jamba. If you're playing with your heart and not just your wallet, it's difficult to give your all for multiple sponsors.
- No mega-star baggage allowed. Our sports partners need to strive for achievement in the same way as our consumers and we do.

"Ultimately, we want the hearts and minds of real patriots to join us in a brand cause," he concluded. "We expect that consumers are going to demand more and more of this authenticity from brands. Jamba is going to stay at the forefront of this development."

The validity of *showing* behaviors versus *telling* ideas is what fuels the buzz about word-of-mouth marketing (WOM). When bloggers use a new gizmo, they talk about it, and thus communicate via their behavior. Much of WOM is not so sincere, however, as most companies practice it as *pay-for-say programming*: there is nothing authentic about trying to pay people off, whether they're movie stars, rappers, or the mom next door who wants to make a few extra bucks shilling products she doesn't use or care about. When record promoters try to bribe radio station DJs to play songs, it's called *payola,* and it's illegal. Most of WOM is monetized on the same criteria, and its model can be self-defeating, because it depends on *natural* networks of comment and response that, by definition, cease to be natural when corporations start paying for inclusion.

If companies behaved honestly, why would they need WOM middlemen?

Today's guerrilla marketers also use behavior as a tactic. For instance, branding that allows consumers to *complete* the branding message works better than presenting completed statements. When T-Mobile launched its myFaves campaign in 2007, the company's offer to let you call your top five numbers for free prompted you to think of who those five would be in your life. The ads made you do something.

Contrast that with the very witty Verizon ads that ran at the same time, promising great service and support because "It's the network." *Yawn.* Doesn't every carrier have a network? And what were consumers supposed to do with this information?

We have a game in our house in which we try to guess what product or service a lifestyle ad is promoting before the punch line gets aired. "Insurance!" my daughter will yell. "No, razor blades!"

my wife counters. "You're both wrong," I announce, "it's air freshener," only to find out the ad is for window-covering treatments.

A similar belief that consumers will internalize scenarios presented to them drives most automotive branding. Viewers are expected to imagine themselves cruising down those interminable, winding roads we see in almost every commercial. Contrast that with branding that requires consumers to *complete it*, like Comcast Digital Cable commercials that cut off actors right before they are obviously going to swear. Sweden's Hive phone service ran a spot a few years ago in which two cameras slowly pulled back to reveal a doofy-looking everyman surrounded by the residue of an orgy: the tagline suggested that when there's a long story to tell, you could use Hive's great rates to call someone. I want to *do something* when I see these ads, not just consume them.

In the ad world, only consuming branding is called *engagement marketing*. In the sales world, it's called *a waste of money*.

I WANT MORE OF ANYTH-*ING*

Speaking of the sales world, there's a truism that goes something like this: "You won't get the sale if you don't ask for it." Most businesspeople know that things rarely happen without an active specific effort to make them happen. You'd get fired if your department's plans relied on fate or happenstance, as branding plans do.

Marketers spend billions with absolutely no expected outcome other than *good feelings* somewhere in the universe. Brands are ideas that simply populate space. We know this because research can survey what people think about so-and-so brand, and deliver very detailed proof of their thoughts.

At that moment.

In that circumstance.

And in response to those questions.

Whether it's what those consumers will think the next moment, as they leave the focus group room, or when they visit a store or website a month later, is pure conjecture (or the opportunity for more costly research). So better add a budget line for *hope* right next to the branding expenditure. And teach your team how to cross their fingers.

Everything else your company does is held to a far higher, more stringent and literal standard. Corporate actions are taken to prompt *reactions*, classified by various internal departments: response, activity, feedback, edit, bid, application, or—gasp—*purchase*. Guerrillas have more in common with the rest of the organization than with branding departments. They prompt actions. Guerrilla marketing has become the noun of branding.

Today's only successful brands are verbs.

Corporations ask nothing of branding other than glorified name recognition.

President Reagan famously asked voters, "Are you better off than you were four years ago?" which summarized the behavioral underpinnings of every election campaign: It prompted voter response. Special-interest groups do the same thing in practice: by definition, these brands exist to realize a behavior, whether saving the rain forests or stopping product testing on animals. Issue-based political campaigns are the same, as are groups dedicated to eradicate or serve diseases. *These brands have a purpose*, and it's not to associate with ideas as much as to deliver behaviors. The very existence of these groups and campaigns is to prompt action, from raising money, to getting members to act in other ways.

Guerrilla marketers use your attention to prompt behaviors, not deliver ideas.

Finding similar examples in the corporate world is hard, primarily because of the stranglehold that traditional branding has over planning and company structure. Many corporate mission statements are presented as behavioral goals. Nike's is "To bring inspiration and innovation to every athlete in the world." But companies get caught up in the inanity of branding rules and nomenclature (remember my little story in the introduction). *Mission statements* aren't the same thing as *brand statements*, or *positions*, or *objectives*. One term doesn't fit into one chart in the slide presentation on the brand, but rather into another. Getting the abstractions right is more important than what happens as a result.

It's a wacky world, and it brings to mind when Tom Cruise's character in the 1996 movie *Jerry Maguire* is repeatedly told he'd written a great memo, to which he declares in exasperation, "It was a mission statement!" as if the label changed the content or behavioral prompt. The complex wording that describes which branding terms are and are not kosher serves to stifle creativity and control the debate. It keeps the conversation focused on communications, which are activities that marketers can understand, and the budgets they control.

So instead of behaviors, we get new product launches that *introduce* products and services to consumers. Highly successful branding creates awareness, of a sort, and nothing more.

Nissan's launch of its new Altima sedan in 2006 featured a kid living in his car for a week (commercials, website, virals, blog). It was celebrated as novel, new-media thinking, targeted exactly at the attitudes and interests of Generation Whatever. It led to no sales, unfortunately; just like most brand experiments, about as close as the campaign got to prompting behavior was listing its website. The Nissan launch was a communications success, but a sales failure, and I guarantee that somewhere in the nutty world of branding, someone could make the case *why that's okay*.

What if businesses saw branding strategy like guerrillas do, as a series of behavioral prompts or a chronology of *calls to action*. The Geico campaign of 2006–07 comes to mind; you know, the one with the tagline, "Give us fifteen minutes, and we'll save you up to 15 percent on your car insurance." That line was probably only a tactic, as much of its integrated marketing wasted space and time promoting its talking spokeslizard (there's a celebrity with no associative values whatsoever, but heck, they could pay it in animated bugs). Or the cavemen.

Imagine if converting *X* number of customers was the purpose of that branding campaign? Not just the business plan *behind* or *aside* of it, but *the branding campaign itself*? Its elements could yield any number of real, measurable behaviors to get there: registrants to the website, inquiries to sales desks, whatever. With no follow-on to the great tagline, however, the potential behavior was most likely left dangling.

I have nothing against filling your branding full of fluffy associations and pretty pictures. You just need ground it all in tangible, behavioral outcomes past *nice feelings*. Declaring an interest doesn't translate into a conversation, unless you want your consumers to waste their time talking about your brand instead of doing something about it. I suspect that's the goal of all the oil companies running advertisements that promote themselves as "green."

LET'S GET BACK TO ME

Appealing to self-interest has always been central to the practice of branding. Some would say it's inherent to capitalism itself.

In the early days of propaganda, Ed Bernays not only convinced a generation of women to smoke as an expression of their independence, but accomplished similar "sleight of word" when he helped the bacon association get people to eat large, greasy breakfasts because it would give them more energy than the traditional coffee and toast. The intellectual framework for such work states that human beings possess inherent, mostly unconscious or latent desires for self-satisfaction. People are genetically selfish, and a few generations of branding for hair tonics, fashion, cars, and just about any other consumable seems to affirm this fact. We buy things to improve our image of ourselves, and our reputation among our neighbors.

So branding is defined as reaching those inner states of mind, and then manipulating them. Most businesses define their customers by it, using terms like "aspirations" and "values" to categorize buyers and potential buyers into different target groups. I think it's absolutely true, for the most part. I want to look better than other old guys my age. Taller, too.

We're going to explore its implications throughout this book. Right now, let's look at the concept of *self-interest* in guerrilla marketing.

If we choose to define brands as internal states of mind, and believe that consumers have relationships with brands as expressions of self and ego, then there's a direct conflict with all of today's experience of media. If owning a fancy car makes me who I am, then I don't want my neighbor to buy one. If I find expensive designer clothing items at a store priced for less, I don't want my friends to know necessarily where I found the stuff. Only this is old, "only my hairdresser knows for sure" thinking.

Today, consumer behavior is different. Not only are items purchased based on the input and affirmation of community, but they are shared therein and thereafter. Consumers, both young and old, are increasingly willing and able to assemble any number of branded items, making the personal combinations unique, while rendering the value of any particular brand less exclusive, and certainly not a secret worth keeping.

No single brand defines the consumer, and it isn't enough any longer to promote something that will make me better than my neighbor for buying it. Rather, it must also *make me better for having shared it*.

We do not live by consuming brand alone.

When guerrilla marketers talk to one, they also talk to many.

We come back to the importance and value of behavior as a guiding principle, and those phone calls I made on 9/11. We can label the communications efforts any sort of marketing—engagement, experiential, persuasion—but there needs to be real behavior at both ends of the equation. Again, it's easy to attach your company name to some idiotic snippet of video, or even to overthink it and find resonating depths of meaning in how some kid's haircut embodies the attitudes of your brand. *But there needs to be a deliverable beyond endless delivery*. Viruses have no purpose other than being shared. We businesspeople don't have that luxury. The medium is not the message.

The message is the message.

Some of the best commercial applications of this truism come from businesses that spend zero time and money trying to manage marketing communications, and instead focus on simply prompting those behaviors.

Again, consider the Nike+ website, built on top of the iPod-compliant running shoe distance monitor and tracker (Nike+ Sport Kit). It received little marketing support, relying instead on legitimate, actual word of mouth to drive awareness. Everything about the behavioral prompts supported product purchase and/or use. The service itself encouraged sharing.

Another example would be from Dove, which in 2004 introduced the "Campaign for Real Beauty" with ads featuring what appeared to be real people (i.e., not cosmetically perfect) and a website, charitable fund, and extended applications to other products, such as its Pro-Age line (2007). Not only was the theme intriguing—soap that actually *didn't* promise to do anything better or different than other soaps—but Unilever, Dove's maker, spent a lot of money creating materials that were intended solely for sharing.

It did very little if any selling for the products per se, but hoped that consumers would buy them because they felt good about Dove's position. Had it included more behavior on the back end—like offering people real things to do, say, create, and buy— it would have been a brilliant, copy-worthy success. I've wondered more than once whether the argument that being old and ugly was the same as being an *individual*, and whether or not it resonated with women, it would prompt soap sales. But things were clearly working on that front.

Prompting behaviors turns cause marketing into **purpose marketing**.

Join the team.

Further the issue.

Add. Improve.

Make a real difference, in your life and in that of your fellows.

Just Do It.

Guerrillas know that the value is in the *doing*, not the *saying*. Branding sometimes works best without any of the communications and promotional trappings of traditional marketing.

We did something like this at Nissan back in the late 1990s. Our competitors were making lots of noise about programs to support diversity. We'd sit around a conference table and bemoan the fact that other companies would make inconsequential contributions to a charity, and then spend far more money to place ads promoting their largesse.

Our approach was to fund a real program, and then not tell anybody about it.

Nissan sponsored the HBCU Summer Institute. Every penny went into the program. I don't think they've promoted it to this day, and I believe that it was one of the most meaningful, honest, and powerful programs ever implemented by a company. If you cared about things like this, you knew about it.

There are endless branding applications of the guerrilla approach, not the least of which are on the customer service side of the purchase equation. Does your company give customers something worth talking about after they've bought and used your product or service, or are they *managed* via programs, mostly automated or outsourced, to keep your expenses down? Users might get tremendous value from their purchases. There may be absolutely no problems or issues to resolve. Yet you are missing the true value of their patronage if you're not inspiring and empowering them to be loyal activists. This function, like the branding as behavior approach overall, doesn't belong to marketing, because it has very little to do with what your company says. The color of your logo won't make a difference. The quote in the press release won't move the dial. Incentivizing consumers with a WOM campaign might ruin their credibility, or sour their own enthusiasm. *What matters is behavior*, and you can prompt it anywhere in your organization. Give them behaviors that matter, to them and to your business. Don't just think like an operations person, finance type, or general manager. And don't think like a marketer.

Think like a guerrilla.

A NEW HABIT

Being the new Nike isn't about terrorism, it's about seeing the truism that prompting behavior matters more than creatively delivering image. Today's guerrilla marketers show us that guerrilla marketing has changed, and that the biggest component of that change has been the addition of a behavioral element (or elements) to every step of campaign execution.

It illustrates the new truth that branding without behavior is pretty much purposeless. Just another TV show that nobody's watching. Or an ad everyone ignores. Today's "successful" brand marketers give us little to remember, and nothing to do . . . the least of which is to make a purchase.

There are four major components to the way guerrillas understand brand today:

1. **Ride behaviors, don't create them.** Successful branding activates behaviors we've already considered, so it makes a more compelling impact more quickly, and more often.

2. **Show, don't tell.** Presentation of brand isn't an idea or description, but rather an expression by example. This makes it more believable and real.

3. **Prompt behaviors, not ideas.** We complete our internal conversations about things with our own actions, and by doing so we become associated ("engaged") with a process.

4. **Talk to many, every time you talk.** Successful brands move—not just encourage or allow—their consumers to share, modify, improve, and ask for more touchpoints every time they "touch" branding.

Another way of looking at these factors would be to give them more brand-friendly names, distilling the behavioral truisms of branding to:

1. Habit
2. Example
3. Action
4. Involvement

There is no good reason why every branding campaign shouldn't be structured to deliver these qualities via behaviors, not images and words.

There are lots of bad reasons, though.

Mostly, they're the result of fixed mind-sets and worldviews that are focused on *doing branding* and not on *making sales*. There's no existing structure within most companies from which to develop or manage a behavioral approach to branding. It's just plain easier to allow the marketers to spend money to interview people and create pretty materials. So even if all you get in return are some glossy ads and great collateral materials, you can point to an *it* and say you did what the experts told you to do. You *did branding*. But if there's not a behavior associated with every item you did, whether large or small, what you did was quite possibly waste your money.

Behavior is branding in the real world.

Consumers consume via moments or events that are mutually and chronologically dependent. Just as people don't generally learn a new behavior, they also won't consider amending an old one without credible support for the decision. Purchase actions don't happen unless other behaviors occur first, and loyalty is less a static state and more dependent on recurrence of behaviors. Truly, the sales funnel is really *a set of gated locks*, as if in a canal.

Each must be successfully opened and closed before the next can do the same. All the time.

We'll look at this more in subsequent chapters, but the idea of a *Chronology of Purchase Intent* is key to developing and delivering branding that works. We do things in order. Today's successful branding reflects this, perhaps instinctively.

You've seen the issues facing branding, and the challenges facing your business. Ads no longer compel. Promises aren't believable. It costs more to get less accomplished in the marketplace. Customer loyalty is measured in seconds. The standard, accepted approaches to branding are not equipped to address these issues. They can't break out of the box of their own traditions and biases.

We should be forsaking all the symbolism and reliance on interpretation that's been so central to branding, and instead address habits, engender trust, prompt action, and earn loyalty. Yet many companies are actually doing *more* of the old stuff.

True guerrilla marketers don't; they break all the old rules of branding—including the laws of guerrilla marketing—and prompt behavior, not just awareness. So consider this idea in relation to your business. Don't worry about overarching plans, or how to integrate all the useless verbiage that exists in your marketing department around mission, goals, objectives, or *pomegranates*. See if you can link events or materials to desired actions. Perhaps link two or three, or however many you can. Add an action verb to the next branding campaign, and test to see whether you can get your targets to do something other than be passive recipients of branding brilliance.

Conversely, if something can't link to a behavior, consider dropping it. You can always add it back if your bottom line suffers a hit. It probably won't, though.

So enough about the new Nike. It's time for a *new* new chapter to get written, and it should feature your company's success.

This book is about exploring how (YOUR COMPANY NAME HERE)™ can start writing the rules for others to emulate and try to follow.

CHAPTER 4

The Rise of the Anti-Brand

Imagine if chess players had access to web search.

Chess is a game of possibilities. Each player selects from a rule-based range of choices, which sprouts a tree of subsequent choices depending on what the other player does. The game has a linear direction in time that drives to a predefined conclusion. Thousands of years of experience and thinking support thousands of varying scenarios, many of which have marvelous names, like the Lopez-Gianutio Counter Gambit, the zwischenzug, and Alekhine's gun. The resulting gameplay is quite ordinary—you probably haven't gone to a match and cheered for your favorite grand master lately—because the intrigue and engagement come from the potentiality that precedes and follows each move.

Could a player improve her chances of victory if she called up a search window on her computer, and typed a simple query like "should my rook take the bishop?" Unfortunately, no. Answering it would require lots of detail on all of the other pieces and positions on the board. A search on "what will my opponent do?" would yield gibberish. Even a question such as "to which of four locations should I move my rook?" would need to include the opposing player's knowledge and game style to calculate an answer.

Although web search would be pretty much useless during the game, it's not impossible to program a computer to answer such questions. IBM's Deep Blue supercomputer did it well enough to defeat a world chess champion back in 1997. Programmers spent endless hours telling the machine *what* moves worked *when* and *why*, and it had to be able to process 200 million positions per second. When they put the machine into a game in real time, it outcalculated its way to victory.

Doing a web search on "laundry detergent" or "fluorescent lightbulbs" is also a game of possibilities, only the range of those possibilities makes Deep Blue's intelligence look like that of a slug. Maybe that's one reason why the average consumer search takes eleven minutes.[1] Only one in every ten business users claims to find the information she or he was looking for on the first attempt.[2]

Yet search has forever changed the way consumers behave. It shifts authority from the information-*giver* to the answer-*seeker*, and exposes every conceivable aspect of brands to scrutiny. Even in its early adolescence—it was only ten years ago that Google's founders were still in grad school—it daily puts many millions of people in contact with information they never would have otherwise found. From locating the nearest bakery to finding instructions for building bombs, it has enabled people to find much of what they look for, and sometimes find something else, or more. However imperfect, web search is the lubricant that makes connecting possible for businesses all over the world, not to mention governments, special interest groups, and porn collectors.

That's because web search is the most amazing lead-generation mechanism ever invented. No longer does your business have to wait for all of that brand awareness to trickle *down* to the masses. Search allows interested folks to percolate *up* via their own inquisitiveness and literally ask you to tell them something. This is what experts call *behavioral marketing*, and it references the specific technique of placing a clickable term (or ad) in front of a consumer who has the highest probability (based on past behavior clicking on things) to click on it. It has inherent value, because there's usually a reliable statistical model to correlate X number of clicks with Y number of sales transactions.

Relevance in lead generation isn't chess yet, but more like a game of "pick this card from the deck," and the simple math behind oddsmaking has driven search-related ad spending to increase in double-digit increments above $10 billion since 2006. Worldwide online ad spending is expected to top $80 billion by the year 2011.[3] There is someone out in the cybervoid right now, sitting at a computer or trolling the Internet on her mobile phone, just a click away from buying whatever it is you sell.

You can and should spend money *optimizing* your website; putting cues into your site so it comes up in her search results is something called search engine optimization, or SEO. And you should play around with *buying words*, which means your terms might come up higher on the list of sponsored results that appear along with the presumably unbought, *organic* results.

In a way, you can look at it as reverse direct mail, as the results for B2B marketers have often tracked one another. Business-to-business websites generated a 2.3 percent conversion rate from search-engine-generated traffic as early as the last quarter of 2005.[4] So search is an unbeatable global entry point to your sales/marketing leaky funnel.

It's an electronic fishing net.

Internet flypaper.

But lead generation isn't branding, however. Ask anyone in sales.

Leads emerge *out* of the indecipherable muck of logos and buzzwords that branding propagates into the cosmos. Calling every searcher a lead is kind of like calling each chess player a winner, or every person you pass on the street a potential friend or spouse. That's why giving greater *relevance* to every searcher is the topmost Holy Grail quest within the web 2.0+ community. If online searches get more productive, people will do it more often and more successfully, for more reasons, and require less incentive to do so. Searches will facilitate and address more choices, more *behaviors*, like Deep Blue could provide the right answers to every question in the chess match. And better answers will mean better leads.

But search is far more than an Internet phenomenon. It's a fundamental change in how consumers behave, and recasts how they interact with the world, whether researching term papers, finding relatives or long-lost loves, or buying toothpaste.

Search is a verb that is not restricted to the web. Once embraced, the idea influences *every* interaction. People who get used to *finding* things are far harder to *lead* or *direct*. As consumers are enabled to spend more time *doing* things instead of *thinking*, traditional channels of communication, and what those channels used to declare, become less relevant. Companies require more tools, more interactions, and a better understanding of consumer behavior in order to prompt more sales transactions.

None of this is good for traditional models of brand and branding. If guerrilla marketing shows how behavior can change how a company *sells* things, search is the tool that describes the change in how consumers *buy*.

More search means less brand.

THE BURDEN OF CHOICE

"I'll always drive GM," my dad declared years ago, having just traded in his Delta 88 for whatever latest model GM offered him in exchange. It was just something that he did, like millions of other consumers. They lived up to the expectations of a name or icon of traditional branding, which would embed in consumers some specific information, emotions, or associations. Like a marketer's Manchurian candidate, brand was believed to overpower all other influences, including those from real-life experience. People had relationships with brands, or got "married" to them.[5] Companies spent billions promoting them as shorthand for all the things folks thought, wondered, or needed to know about things. Consumers had few tools with which to do much else than, well, *consume* it all.

Only today, my dad drives a Toyota. He researched his purchase online, and a dear cousin recommended it.

We now know that many of those supposed "brand relationships" on which corporations relied were really nothing more than *habits*, oftentimes unconscious. People paid more for things because they didn't know better. They behaved certain ways because of routine. Brands didn't cause this phenomenon as much as cover up many of its true drivers.

So, while most branding is still based on something that can be said or declared—in a magazine ad, bantered back and forth in an online forum, framed in an inane Internet video, or as a deliverable from a link in web search—people have changed their behavior.

I'd suggest that consumers don't search with questions about brands as much as with generic terms about things or activities. They're not looking for answers *from* brands, but rather answers *about* brands. And the results they get in searches are a far cry from the controlled channel of communications that most companies would hope for anyway:

- Almost half of the top fifty UK grocery brands had detractors in the top ten search results.[6]
- More than 25 percent of search results on Google for the world's twenty largest brands are links to consumer-generated content, not corporate sites.[7]

- Fifteen percent of searches end up at competing brands, suggesting that searchers are looking for something other than branding.[8]

- Brand names rarely, if ever, feature on the top search terms on any of the top search engines.

It also seems that brands often don't matter when it comes to online *purchase* behavior. According to ad-placement company (and Google vassal) DoubleClick earlier this decade, roughly half of all online shoppers conducted related searches before making an online purchase. Out of the average two or more searches, and often four to six (depending on the product category), brand names of online retailers were in the minority of all the purchase-related searches made during shopping research, and were a factor only late in the buying cycle, if at all.[9] Makes you wonder why there's so much money being spent on digital branding.

Choice, it turns out, is not the friend of branding.

Consumer reliance on brands has been replaced by secretive, proprietary mathematical equations, called *algorithms*, which operate behind the scenes at Google, Yahoo!, MSN, Ask, Lycos, Snap, and other web search engines. People enter search terms, and the algorithms provide the connections and associations that corporations assumed, once upon a time, could be made by branding.

Web search undoes these connections and treats brands as *words*, just like in the Middle Ages: marks with no implicit meanings beyond those that an anonymous public of Internet users, and secret algorithms, choose to give to them. What's connecting people to products and services is not a direct relationship with corporate marketing, but rather the independent, user-prompted behaviors of search.

So this tool isn't just a lead generator, it's *a constant emergency exit or trapdoor out of your brand.*

It's worse than that, actually, because web search exists as a siren call to check, shop, affirm, or debate every little thing your business says or does. Search serves as the chaperone, watchdog, and conscience doppelgänger to every corporation trying to do business in the twenty-first century.

I just completed a search for "tuna fish," a perennial lunchtime favorite where I come from. The first listing on the results page was for an image of a worm, linked to text about "Helminth Parasites Grouped by Location in Host," followed by:

- A link to a commercial tuna fishing industry website
- A Wikipedia entry on the fish of the family Scombridae
- Two recipe sites
- An e-commerce site for an expensive electronics device

Typing "what canned tuna should I eat?" yielded an entire page of reasons why I shouldn't eat it at all, courtesy of environmental, women's health, and other special-interest groups with a net to shred about fishing. Finally, I entered the brand name Starkist, and got the company's website, where I mostly found stories about its marketing. The other results had lots on political issues.

What is accessible to consumers via search is infinitely variable, and ultimately out of your control. It enables a repository of corporate information and history that replaces your brand narrative with a constantly growing and evolving space wherein people find context and truth about your business. Ultimately, this history forms independently of your traditional branding and communications efforts.

Just look at the many years Procter & Gamble has spent trying to dispel the belief that its old corporate logo is the sign of the devil. American Airlines is arguably a highly searched term (as are most major travel-related entities), yet a third-party site appears on the first page of search results, listing details on fatal crashes since 1970.

Search is more proof that there are no longer any one-way channels through which you can talk to consumers, or that branding has nothing to do with telling people what to think. You just can't do it. Opinions change, prioritizations shift, and the consumer path to purchasing a product or service starts to look a lot like that evolving tree of possibilities sprouting in front of a chess player. Search behavior dimensionalizes the time and order qualities of that tree, that Chronology of Purchase Intent. *Brand is now a set of user-prompted behaviors,* or moments, in which consumers ask, learn, compare, or do something else.

If only it were as simple as hanging out a sign and waiting for searchers to find your business. There's that one person right now ready to buy from you, for sure. But the vast majority of other searchers are at different points along their pathways to buy. Every time they use search is a unique moment when at least five qualities other than the terms they enter into their web browsers impact their experience and subsequent decisions:

1. **Context.** The physical and virtual qualities surrounding and supporting the search query are important, from time of day to what else is going on, both in the real world and online. Search doesn't know whether you're playing chess, or any other game . . . or playing no game at all.

2. **Timing.** Is the person looking to make a purchase imminently, just starting to fish around on a thought that barely qualifies as an idea, or somewhere between those two end states? Oh,

and those two poles are different for each user, and usually moving.

3. **Predisposition.** This represents the things the searcher knows and believes, and her or his aversion to risk, as well as colors, proper names, or any other of the infinite qualities that make one human being different from another. So the capacity to understand *the counsel of search* varies by individual.

4. **Competition.** What have the consumer's other searches yielded, whether from competing companies, critics, or other entities? Imagine if the last search result told you to ignore the next one, or the results two searches ago no longer appeared when you wanted to recheck (and forgot to bookmark or tag them).

5. **Purpose.** There are no rules to the game as far as search understands, so it's just as likely that the searchers don't know exactly what they're looking for, as it is that they're looking for anything at all.

This is the challenge to making web search relevant to chess players and dishwasher purchasers alike. It would be great if it could literally read people's minds, and operate with all of the human ingenuity that Kasparov sensed as his chess game went down in flames. But purchase decisions are often irrational, as we saw in chapter 2. We faulty human beings tend to make imperfect decisions.[10] A smart corporate decision would be to skip hoping that relevance in web search will overcome these obstacles anytime soon. Relevance to these behaviors is as much the responsibility of corporate strategy as it is the job of search firm algorithms and computer banks. No technical advancement can completely address or overcome these facts.

There's no *there* there in search, no place to put your brand as a static *thing* that marketing experts have designed. Search doesn't operate in the language of colors and buzzwords. It doesn't exist unless someone dips into it, almost like a quantum physics moment: consumers conjure it into being by stepping through one of a limitless number of doors, at a limitless number of different moments in time. Web search then aggregates, from all of the potential information available online, to create search results. It's a snapshot of a moment.

Search takes a picture far better than the human mind could ever recall, and it's more efficient in accessing the breadth and depth of information available to it. It does everything we'd hoped individuals *used* to do with all of the crapola we used to throw at them, only now they prompt it themselves, and an independent, irascibly unpredictable, and uncontrollable machine consciousness finds the content for them, based in large part on the behaviors of their fellow searchers.

Search is half the equation; what happens next is the real opportunity.

We've seen the implications of search in the business and political spheres, as job candidates lose employment opportunities because a simple web query called up their favorite diversions listed on their Facebook page, or the set of spring break photos that only anonymous online close friends were supposed to see on WebShots. The reach of search makes every candidate for political office into a liar, or at least renders even the slightest mistake or slip of the tongue visible as if it were a position on an issue that actually mattered in the real world. This is the real *long tail* that trails after every company.

And whether consumers interact with your business online, on the phone, via store visit, through product use, or via string and paper cups, no amount of branding can change the fact that *search is the anti-brand.*

ASK, AND YE SHALL FIND

My mouth hung open in awe as I was walking the aisles of the O'Reilly Web 2.0 convention in San Francisco, past row after row of booths promoting technical tools and services for online business, marketing, and communications. Many of the technologies on display had never even occurred to me before. To a geek reared on novels by Isaac Asimov and TV news coverage of Apollo moon shots, this sort of stuff is the work of gods. I left the session feeling utterly jazzed, electrified with the belief that machines can do anything.

But machines don't make purchase decisions. People do. And as I shook the blinding crush for my mechanical bride from my mind, it became clear to me that the biological and behavioral aspects of web search, like those of all technology solutions, would be more important to brand and business planning than the Cyranos of devices would ever have us believe.

Search is a larger, behavioral reality that impacts corporate strategy.

The inevitability of new technology is a fact with which every business must contend. But technologists have a bias when they answer questions of how humans function. Machines and systems are not just enablers of behavior, but can be prompts, environments, boundaries, and overall controllers. *When people act on their intentions, it's called behavior.* When the novelist George Eliot wrote, "The strongest principle of growth lies in human choice," she was referencing human development and the potential for improvement and change.[11] One could argue that these qualities are the real target for branding via search. Thoughts about brands or technologies on our desktops, in our ears, or surrounding us in the ether don't actualize that potential. It's choice that does it.

Behavior is the ultimate statement of brand, and search is a tool that transforms all of those moments of consumer contemplation into action. Decision-making that we once consigned to ethereal thought, removed from the prying eyes of marketers outside of the qualitative questions asked about it via focus groups and polls, becomes behavioral and measurable.

There needs to be conversation at your company about search that involves you and other operational departments, as well as the brand marketers. And there are at least seven strategic points about search—irrespective of the latest technology miracle that is or soon will be marketed to you—that your team should consider, debate, refute, or replace.

First, **technological development is going to continue.** There's just too much money to be made linking people and information, and the fact that only 1.2 percent of consumers make a purchase from a website on their original search session suggests that there's a lot more business to be had.[12] The endpoint of this development is truly the stuff of science fiction. Imagine having infinite, absolutely current knowledge available to you at every waking moment, infusing thoughts and decisions far beyond chess moves with the experience and counsel of countless centuries. The French mathematician Pierre-Simon Laplace pondered a time when mankind would know all of the possible positions of every atom and then, effectively, be able to predict the future. I think Google has embraced this idea of *facilitated everything* as an actual business objective.

In the meantime, two things to remember:

First, you're going to be told, or you're going to tell someone, that web search is *part science, part art*. This is gobbledygook to cover up the fact that nobody can explain exactly what's going on. Try to focus on the *science* part and not waste your money on the *art* part. Be critical of the statistics. Look askance at your search numbers, and bear in mind that a leading pay per click (PPC) firm (earning money each time a site visitor clicks on an ad) found that a third of the most active companies buying search terms didn't know the total financial value of the resulting sales.

Second, search has a built-in wall for addressing it head-on, because the proprietary inner workings of the engines are ultimately unknowable. Consumer behavior is the only real way to measure it, so try and find ways to track what people do beyond clicking on your term or link. There's a chance that your investment in search could qualify as one of your largest single marketing spends, so consider this a business-wide strategy, not a technology tool.

The next point to ponder is that **search is going to change dramatically**. It seems that one of the primary keys to delivering relevance for current behavior is for providers to possess more knowledge of past behavior. This effort is advancing by leaps and bounds, building upon Microsoft's announced plans in 2007 that it would better track search habits, so as to place ads more closely aligned with search queries.[13] Yahoo!'s Panama project was designed to do the same thing.[14] Google has long stored historic usage of its web browser, which can similarly help tee up targeted ads.[15] Expect more.

Advances in this functionality may raise interesting questions about the trade-offs consumers will be willing to make for quicker, better search results. Perhaps folks will create different *avatars* much like they do in the social media, and use them for different search purposes. Experts have written about the *online disinhibition effect*, referencing a number of splintered, boundaryless behaviors that emerge when people can experience the web anonymously.[16]

Conversely, perhaps people won't care at all about becoming *known* and losing their anonymity. Ultimately, search providers make their money from commercial exploitation, and as long as that exploitation comes across as helpful, all will be well.

Search these days isn't about consumers finding products, but rather **products finding consumers**.

Anonymous or not, you can expect that your competition will try to use search to find consumers in ever smarter ways. Ad placement will get better, so we'll see ever fewer ads cluttering up search pages. Searches within e-commerce sites will get ever better at dynamic presentation, so products will appear, in a certain order, featuring pricing that is partially dependent on visitor, overall visits, and other trend data.

Search will continue to expand to other media beyond the web:

- Leading European telecoms are developing search capability for mobile phones; in the UK alone, 20 percent of phone subscribers have access to mobile Internet at broadband speeds, and that number will only grow.[17]

- U.S. carriers started following suit midway through 2007, and search is growing on phones in China.

- I can already search restaurants on my cable TV, which has been common in parts of Europe for years.

For that matter, search happens every time someone drives down the street or walks into a brick-and-mortar store. There are technologies that enable businesses to track that behavior—where people walk, how long they stand in a spot, and where they go next—so as to better allocate items, set prices, or actualize any other geophysical corollaries of search results. How you engage in this broad development—beyond online search via a computer—will be as important as how you optimize your website for search terms.

Third, **_greater relevance will bring hiccups._** Search today is like broadcast media was during the 1950s heyday of mass media: it endeavors to be all things to all people, servicing every search query with some threshold of usefulness. In this way, it's in the Gilligan's Island phase of content relevance. Results are often a lowest-common-denominator deliverable, hoping to please most people most of the time. This too shall pass. If it tracks with the evolution of entertainment media, web search may trade size of audience served for greater relevance and utility.

Multiple cable TV channels already deliver specialized content to specialized groups of viewers. Every hobby or affliction has dozens of websites or blogs dedicated to it, just like it used to have its own print magazine. This fragmentation of target audiences has been both an issue and an opportunity for traditional marketers, and it could be replicated in the search area. Be prepared that trolling for interested consumers might get more rarefied, and commensurately more expensive.

Or be prepared for a backlash. _Transparency_ is a mostly unavoidable trend in business, and it's a two-way street. Trade secrets, proprietary technologies, special sauces, and any number of other legal or procedural conventions usually go the way of the dodo. Sometimes it's a purposeful transition, while other times it's simply the wear of use and time. The algorithms that run search engines may be no exception.

Think about it: Relevant search requires ever greater amounts of information from the searcher, whether consciously given or automatically tracked. Yet there's no reciprocal revelation from the search providers. Algorithms are secret, so there's really no complete, verifiable way for consumers to know that the search results with which they're served are both _unbiased_ and _accurate._ These conclusions must be taken as acts of faith, and faith is not a dependable quality in commerce. Perhaps consumers will start _selling their attention,_ using tools to collect records of their online behavior, and then selling them to interested marketers.

People could just as easily challenge the overall dynamic of search because they see violations of its agnosticism and accuracy. Major companies, such as Saab and BMW, have been caught trying to artificially raise their page ranking results by hosting false or forwarding sites (*cloaking* is a way to rig search results, and it got BMW Europe banned from appearing in Google search listings in 2006).[18] Informal secondary markets exist for businesses that want to control use of search terms, and pay resellers, distributors, or other interested parties to forsake bidding on them. A squabble in 2007 in the UK revealed how eBay sellers fix auctions by bidding up one another's offerings.[19]

Perhaps mainstream consumers will never catch on to these shenanigans—I'm not sure Saab's or BMW's brand equity has suffered a loss in eyeballs, or ohms, or however it's measured—but these sorts of facts could, over time, tend to disenchant some of the most valuable, high-worth consumers to whom corporations would love to use search to sell. And one story, at just the wrong time, could prompt a flashmob of public opinion, which could cause major pain for the search community.

Will faith in agnostic and accurate search survive as search relevance improves?

Fourth, *alternate searches will be part of the growth*. "For many people, 60 percent search accuracy isn't good enough, so while I love Google, vertical search is inevitable," explained Silicon Valley venture capitalist and blogger Paul Kedrosky. "It's a challenge to do it right, but we're going to see more branded searches."

Vertical and *social* search are two such alternate, or specialized, search environments:

1. **Vertical search** is a focused version, founded upon a specific subject. So when you want to find an airplane ticket, you can go to travel-dedicated sites, like Travelocity or Orbitz, and the computer searches only web information about airlines. Then the secret algorithms decide what to show to you. The idea is that this search is faster and deeper, and thus a better version of broad, generic search.

2. **Social search** utilizes a sort of community that organizes around a subject, like TripAdvisor for travel information, or Etsy for an alternative for auctions. Users post their personal experiences and opinions, so the searching relies on no secret algorithm to rank results, but rather the prioritizations of real people. Yahoo! Movies provides something similar for movie reviews. So does Cars.com, as do many technology store sites. Wikipedia presents content that is developed in a communal way.

You may want to consider the intriguing possibilities for incorporating these varieties of search behavior in support of your business.

Up to now, the marketing approach has been to see these refined search approaches as channels for advertising—you've heard this rant many times, I know—so if there's a search specializing in fingernail care and your company makes fingernail clippers, then what a great place to run a banner ad. But banner ads do poorly most everywhere, as this approach fails to recognize the behavioral purpose of search.

Imagine instead a marketing plan that encouraged your customers to rate and post their experiences with your products or services. How about creating a branded search for your industry category, where people could find valuable information on you *and on your competitors*, all thanks to your corporate beneficence? If the idea is to influence behaviors and not solely thoughts, then why aren't the FAQs on your website—either customer issues or corporate info highlights—ranked by frequency, then promoted as an honest reflection of real consumer action? The UK's Sainsbury's and Thomson have had great success sponsoring search on Yahoo! Answers.[20]

There are rich implications for using search as a paradigm for organizing internal information for use by your employees and partners. These are audiences who crave transparency and knowledge. Search, properly configured, can deliver it, as mainstream marketers like Procter & Gamble and OfficeMax have proven with sponsorship of communities for interested consumers. If only they'd not organized these connections around brand blather, and instead focused on legitimately supporting search-relevant needs.

Fifth, the evolution in search *will force companies to think a lot more about being found*. Imagine that somebody clicks on the search term that you've spent good money to buy. Okay, that's one way they'll find you. Perhaps your link appears in a social forum, or gets posted by a blogger with a grudge. For that matter, a consumer simply types your website URL into a browser after seeing it printed on the side of your product, or makes a phone call into your customer care center. Or maybe he asks a question of a friend who happens to be one of your employees, or who works at a partner or vendor. Maybe somebody interviews at your HQ for a job, and becomes a sounding board for friends who have questions or comments about your business.

Search is the consumer tool that transforms your brand from static, outbound statement to changing, two-way behavior.

Ponder this dynamic for a minute. Somebody seeks your business out—via whatever medium or forum that's available to them—which means they've *done something*. They've behaved in a certain way. A zillion things may have crossed their minds during the day, but there is room for only a limited number of actions, and actualizing the thought relevant to your business somehow got to the top of the list, even if for a brief, perhaps low-involvement moment. Even if you know where they *came from* via a search engine, you have no idea where they are in their own personal journeys through a Chronology of Purchase Intent, or their chess games of life.

The branding traditionalists will say that this is the reason your communications need to be *integrated* across all *touchpoints*. Your brand needs to appear the same way irrespective of how, when, or where your customers or potential customers seek. Walk-ins to the car showroom need to get the same glossy brochures; callers to your 800 number get the same cross-sell propaganda when they are parked in hold. We all should stare numbly at the same TV ads, whether allocated nationally or locally. You know the drill.

This is backwards. Giving every searcher the same destination is like buying the same size clothes for them. Or calling them all Fred. And I don't care if Fred is the name of your best product, either.

Relevant search presumes that your business can be relevant, so that means that thinking about what to give consumers in response to their search queries, irrespective of how they're delivered to you, is as important as triggering them in the first place. And fantasizing that anyone wants to have a "conversation with your brand" is silly.

Consider such chess moves as:

- **Odysseus's Intent.** Are you sending searchers to the right places? Your corporate website home page is rarely the best destination for incoming inquiries. Certainly, what you put on it should mirror the most common reasons people seek it out (versus your favorite creative branding du jour). Since much of the conversation about the world occurs outside your corporate control, could you choose to send certain searchers to external destinations, such as conversation or community sites? Maybe someone you hope is exploring your product category should go to a community where you have great standing first, instead of you hitting them over the head with your corporate propaganda. So Chrysler buys a thousand search terms in mid-2007, only to link them to their commercial videos. It answers users' search with ads? How inane.

- **The Polymath Amble.** Are you trying to give too many answers simultaneously? My mortgage lender has the most frustratingly complex interactive voice response system, or IVR. It forces me to wade through series after series of menus, requiring me to identify with ever greater clarity what it is I'm looking for. This is just dumb: couldn't a search ranking tool identify the most common inquiries in any given time period, or perhaps from a specific geography, as a starting point? The same goes for many of the menus on websites, which are organized on the principle of what a company wants to tell people, not what people want to know. Integrated communications theory says that if I searched online because I saw a TV ad (I know, it rarely works this way), the first thing I should do on the website I find in my search . . . is see the ad again! It's *integrated. Get it?* Why isn't there a link to a noted, fair-minded external community of users (or watchdogs) on the mortgage site, for instance?

- **Alternate Ending.** What are the behaviors you provide or require? My credit card company requires me to enter my ten-digit card number when I call, and then the live service representative demands that I repeat it, as if they want to challenge my very desire to search for information. Do people have to enter names or e-mail addresses in order to access certain searchable information about your business? I know that makes perfect sense to the customer relationship management (CRM) folks who are struggling to prove some worth to your business, but it's often a declarative message to visitors that you want them to do something *for you,* versus your business doing something *for them.*

Sixth, you might want to consider that **utilizing search is more about asking questions than answering them**. More than a century of expert branding has yielded trust in corporations that is at an all-time low. Europe and the United States seem to trade positions as leaders in this free fall.[21] The idea that anyone is searching for what a company has to say, let alone what it has to say about brands, is just not reasonable. There's a specific product information step required in many purchase chronologies, especially as the entry price and/or complexity of operability of the product or service goes up. But lots else can, and perhaps should, be effectively outsourced to the individuals, communities, and other resources that serve to inform and affirm products and services. Web search suggests that one of the most important things your business can do for search is to prompt or assist with meaningful *questions*, instead of trying to provide all of the *answers*.

I've taken this approach proactively in my life, and I used it for this book. In addition to posing a list of prepared questions in my interviews with experts around the world, I added one final question: "What should I have asked you?" I often got the best and most challenging thinking from this question. Many times, I got additional questions that I needed to explore.

Is it more credible for businesses to pose questions to help searchers find answers? BP has been running its environmentally friendly branding for a few years now, yet it poses questions that it then presumes to answer. I'm not sure that the most realistic-looking corporate video can overcome inherent (and perhaps well-placed) suspicions about Big Oil answering questions about the environment. They just don't have the authority to do it.

While supermarkets are the industry category that consumers feel is generally trustworthy and honest, with a whopping 34 percent ranking according to one poll, oil companies rate at the bottom of the list, at 3 percent. Were any of them to embrace the alternative approach, search might link instead to an actual green group that could talk independently and honestly about Big Oil's activities. This approach, incorporated into overall communications strategy, might provide a way to understand and address the spot at which any individual might be in his or her Chronology of Purchase Intent—revealed by their choice of additional questions—as well as a chance to position your business to do things in response to what the searcher has done in order to find you.

Posing a question proactively affords you the possibility of offering to take action to help answer it. Send a report, calculate a hypothetical, link to further resources . . . these are all behaviors that a business can prompt, and thus speak back to consumers in the language of action that web search demands. CRM should enable this. Relationships are about action, not thought.

Seventh, *behavior can be the key to capturing the true potential of search*. Let's presume the following:

- Web search, along with the general feeling of empowerment that most consumers possess, will never go away, but rather will become a ubiquitous aspect of their (and our) lives.

- Loyalty is not only as fleeting as *what have you done for me lately* would suggest, but is even more tenuously dependent on *what my community thinks about it* or *what it says about what you did for the next customer*. This, too, will only grow over time.

- Consumers will live in a near-constant state of action, ready to actualize a behavior—*looking*, if nothing else—that can, at any given moment, be a defining moment that puts them into a chronology toward their purchase from you or from one of your competitors (or away from any purchase at all).

This *world of perpetual search* makes the old definitions of brand sound almost quaint. Brand cannot somehow keep consumers oblivious to the influences and choices now available to them. Hoping to interject brand between consumers and what they want to explore, share, purchase, and experience disregards the behavioral framework of web search, if not the entire context of commerce and overall experience in the twenty-first century.

Web search is an incredible gift, because it serves as a mechanism to force the actualization of possibilities: once a business decides that behavior matters more than thought, an entirely new operational strategy becomes apparent. The role of your brand is no longer to declare or state anything, but rather to anticipate, prompt, and support the search behaviors of would-be consumers, as well as the requirements of your existing ones.

Search makes expectations about brand real, transforming intents into behaviors, against which you can deliver behaviors in response (and in advance, for that matter). The goal shouldn't be to provide a home or conclusion, but rather to be prepared to constantly participate in searching. Every time a consumer returns to you, he or she is reaffirming your branding. Play it forward.

This means that your e-commerce team cannot develop your search strategy in a vacuum. It certainly won't alone handle its implementation. Search is a concept that exists beyond the confines of the little monitor or mobile phone screen on which you see it. Your strategy should be based on the behavior of would-be and current consumers. The Chronologies of Purchase Intent in which you participate will likely encompass many ways to search for information about your business.

Think about bringing search to your customer. Widgets are little apps that run on computers and allow you to send info to your customers when it's available. It's *found* action, not search. Delivering such substantive behaviors for each of your consumers' contemplated moves could come from departments across your organization.

While researching this book, I committed a cardinal sin on an airplane flight: I started a conversation with my seatmate. The guy next to me was working on his computer, and a lot of familiar Fortune 500 company names kept popping up. I couldn't resist and, to make a long windup short, he turned out to be Dr. Larry Ponemon, founder and leader of the Ponemon Institute, which specializes in understanding online privacy and responsible information management. He was kind enough to talk to me.

"Trust is earned and has a monetary value," he explained. "Online, this is established and tested by what type of site you possess, do you ask permission for additional information, do you authenticate, provide password restore, provide clear answers to questions, and let your customers turn off marketing if they so choose?"

He continued, "Anonymity and trust are in conflict, and right now we have a lot of web traffic driven by the former. But the latter is an inherent vital quality to business relationships. All the talk about privacy online is really a subset of trust, and we're going to see a lot of development in this area. It matters."

Just like in the real world. Web search is a great tool to help us get our heads around the model of brand is behavior, and to expand that thinking to include search as a central consumer behavior. The real world is the domain for that seeking. It doesn't matter that the days of ubiquitous search are far off, or that in the meantime it's just a tool we use sporadically during the day. There still are a multitude of prompts that get people to search, and subsequent behaviors they evidence as a result. How programs are developed and integrated to both participate in this behavior (support it credibly) and siphon people toward your own business Chronologies of Purchase Intent are the central opportunities before your business right now.

Nobody *thinks* their way to winning a chess match, any more than you make money when your consumers think about your business. Relevance doesn't belong to web search; it originates in your business and in the behaviors of your consumers. Let the technologists and entrepreneurs invent improvements to search engine algorithms, and find new ways to deliver information to people's phones or pagers, or directly into their guts.

It'll kill your old brand, but it's a chance for you to invent it anew.

It's your move.

CHAPTER 5

The Myth
of the Consumer/Producer

I thought my viral videos were absolutely brilliant.

It was early 2005 and my client, a global carbonated beverage business, wanted to sell more products to teenagers and young adults. I'd proposed we throw all of the rules of traditional advertising out the window and create three spots: a burping contest, a kid getting sprayed in the face with soda pop, and video gamers distracted by loud farts. The production quality would look like a kid had put it together in his parents' basement. The gags would be tailor-made for YouTube. I couldn't think about the spots without laughing.

My first opportunity to present the finished work to the client took me to a conference room in Europe filled with smart people whom I knew well. I gave my spiel about the brave new future of communications, and on how people both young and old were taking control of marketing as *producers*, not just as consumers. I boldly declared that we had to create material that would not only entertain but prompt people to share it and perhaps create their own. Everyone nodded as I loaded the movies. As soon as I heard the first burp rumble on the conference room speakers, I chuckled, confident that the stuff was just spot-on.

Nobody else laughed. I quickly moved to the second spot, sure that it would get a reaction when the kid got his first face-full of soda pop. *Nothing.* I loaded the final segment—the farting that was destined to bring down the house—and stood paralyzed as the audience shifted uncomfortably in their seats.

"So, whaddayathink?" I asked, my heart in my throat.

"Really, *really* funny," answered one of the marketing guys in a monotone voice. "But what's the point?"

Easy question, I thought. The whole point of the strategy was that *it had no point.* The spots were all about attention, and had nothing to do with selling. We'd reduced the conversation we had with our consumers to a Three Stooges skit, and made the product a setup for a doody joke. By the time we'd talked it through, how-ever, the entire premise seemed like nonsense. Nobody ever saw the spots after that day. The phenomenon of *user-created content* continued on without us.

It's an incredible trend, driven mostly by teenagers and the technically aware, who are inspired by the idea that they have something to say, and find empowerment by the technology that makes it possible to create, publish, and share online. Most of the text, sound, and videos (weblogs, or *blogs,* and their video counter-parts, *vlogs,* audio podcasts, and viral videos) come from individu-als contributing to a new renaissance of mostly low art.

YouTube, which was founded in early 2005 to let anybody share videos with anybody else, had by the same time a few years later grown to command *more than half a percent of all Internet vis-its in the United States,* and over one-third of all the visits to sites in the entertainment/media category. Lots of other sites followed, as did services to let individuals easily share what they'd written or photographed. Chances are you've received a funny video link in your e-mail in-box today, or on your phone. Perhaps you've sent one. If there's a kid in your house under the age of eighteen, she or he is all over it.

You can't have escaped seeing or reading references to such now historic segments as the Coke and Mentos exploding bottle experiments; lonelygirl15's video diary; the debut of *Saturday Night Live*'s "Lazy Sunday" skit on YouTube; the Comcast cable guy asleep while on hold; even the videos of laptop batteries catching fire in hotel conference rooms. Consumers have proven that they have the technology, interest, and available time to create and share content. *Time* magazine announced that its 2006 "Man of the Year" was *You*, meaning the control of media content had shifted from the folks collected into organizations that make and sell stuff for a profit, to disorganized individuals who make and share it for free.

User-created content levels the media field, figuratively and literally.

Talk about a disaster for traditional branding.

Not only are people generally more suspicious and critical of advertising than ever before, but now they can mess it all up. It seems that the media conduit—the foundational tool for sellers to tell buyers what they should think—has been severed, only to be replaced by a complex, undulating web of connections that renders buyers into sometime sellers, sellers into sometime buyers, and lots of people into participants and voyeurs with no business purpose whatsoever. Experts try to qualify this trend as the democratization of media, but the indications are that it is more of the *anarchification* of it.

It turns out that this low art renaissance blurs the differentiation between *professional* and *amateur*, and reveals that the distinction we used to make between the two was due to the limits of old technology. A flourishing *continuum of art* has emerged, created on home computers more powerful than the gizmos that flew the astronauts to the moon, and distributed via the Internet to spots on the globe to which even FedEx won't deliver:

- Projects such as the *Broken Saints* anime series could have never been produced or marketed a decade earlier, but by 2001 the brooding pieces had broken new ground and found an online audience willing to pay for the programs.[1]

- The various Xiao Xiao stick-figure fighters—"hangman" sort of line drawings punching and shooting each other—spawned a cottage industry of entertaining Flash animation shorts.[2]

- Some of the early movie trailer remixes (*mash-ups*) were quite polished, like *The Shining* recut as a comedy, or *Sleepless in Seattle* cast as a horror movie.

- Enterprising gamers continue to take footage from video games and create scripts and soundtracks for cinematic shorts (also known as *machinima*).

The fan-created content component of this phenomenon deserves a brief special mention.

Websites featuring additional scenes from the movie *Titanic* or the Vampire Lestat novels—lovingly posted by fans—attract visitors who consume the material far more regularly and passionately than they ever did network TV sitcoms, or commercials. The universe of Star Trek fan content is particularly immense, with groups of people taking specific elements of the original series and creating extended plotlines that fill in the backstory of the series.[3]

Independent music is another type of user-created content, in that it empowers people to *make* songs instead of just *listen* to them. Not only has technology made sharing songs easier than falling out of bed, but it has enabled thousands of musicians to be heard, and sometimes even make a buck from the exposure. Sites like garageband.com let people post their homemade music and get feedback, while hearing and ranking others. DJs regularly remix every song available to them, creating new versions (and new life) for all types of music.

If search is the anti-brand, is user-created content the anti-search?

By the start of 2008, the phenomenon had gone mainstream. Middle-aged people were following the younger, early content creators, continuing a trend tracing back to earlier this century.[4] It was more common than ever for people of all ages and interests to call-in to radio shows, vote on television programs, or make their interests known by punching an SMS code into their mobile phones. A variety of corporate projects had emerged, from virtual showrooms in Second Life and crazy *American Idol*–like contests for the creation of commercials, to ersatz member pages on social networking sites evoking memories of MySpace.

These activities have been frequently cited as potential lifesavers for the old model of brands: The argument is that consumers are less the recipients of branding, and now more the producers and *co-owners* of it. People will use their newfound powers of creation to reverse their retreat away from branding begun in the 1960s, and instead make more of it, much like a perpetual motion device would generate more power than it consumes.

It's the great hope of making branding once again relevant and worth the many billions of dollars that could be spent on it in the years to come.

But it's just a myth.

EXQUISITELY VAGUE

"If you can't beat 'em, join 'em," the old saying goes, and it sums up the response of the most daring marketers to the changing nature of the mediascape.

Web 2.0.

Consensual conversation.

Buzz, or word of mouth.

User-generated content or branded entertainment.

Social media.

Giving up the brand, and hiring brand evangelists.

If you're involved in a conversation that uses any of these buzzwords, you're likely to get hit with a proposal to spend money on it. It'll include numbers on demographics and involvement that make the possibility of the myth seem as exciting as an unlimited spending tab in Vegas.

Whether voiced or not, the argument behind the myth is that *branding can be refashioned to become content*, and thus be seen by consumers as yet more creative material, no different from the plot of a drama on TV, the characters in a sitcom, or footage of somebody's boyfriend sleeping on a couch. Giving branding content up to this new network is the best way to get the people to see and use it.

But there are a few catches that you won't hear unless your conversation comes with its very own fine print:

- Content is inherently more credible if it makes no claims to credibility.

- Relevance is directly proportional to authenticity, and indirectly proportional to expectation.

- Only the stuff that is apparently worthless possesses any value.

- Therefore, there's no good way to know if it ever helps you *sell anything*.

So much of this thinking echoes the doublespeak we heard only a decade ago, when businesses fell for the idea that they didn't have to make money so much as "capture eyeballs," and networks of corporate alliances and partnerships could trade logos and golf events without ever extracting payment from actual customers. We celebrated much of the branding during those heady days, although few of us now recollect names like pets.com, go.com, or Webvan. Great fortunes were won and lost based on an alchemical equation that would somehow transform the lead of web visits into commercial gold. It never happened for 99 percent of the corporate patients so treated, though it certainly enriched many of the alchemists behind it.

User-created content is the wrong answer to the right question.

The Myth of the Consumer/Producer prompts a similar hope, but with this twist: No longer will marketers have to sell to consumers at all. Rather, *consumers will brand to each other.* No longer is the intent to get consumers to think a certain way about a brand, but rather to give them the materials to think whatever they want. *Search* has them in control of locating information, so the myth suggests they should find more branding that has little to no content or contextual link to a real product or service per se. If it's entertaining, it can and should be branded, impervious to the base qualities of product features or benefits.

If you think this sounds exquisitely vague, you're onto something. The Myth of the Consumer/Producer is beautiful because it allows for the full realization of branding as an activity good for branding's sake alone. It has prompted two broad corporate strategies:

1. **Branding as corporate-created content.** In the 1950s, Procter & Gamble and Colgate-Palmolive would position ads, sponsorship mentions, and even faux news interviews about their products on daytime TV soap operas. As we approach the end of the first decade of the twenty-first century, companies are swapping that sponsorship for either producing the content itself, creating programs that weave elements of branding associations into the programs themselves, or, thanks to the Internet, taking full control of the creation and distribution, like a TV network.

   If you were a fan of the TV show *24* a few years ago, you could watch *The Rookie: CTU*, a series of additional shows that borrowed the settings and context of the original program, much like the fan-created *Star Trek* episodes lifted the *Enterprise*'s phasers and go-go boots.[5] The site was plastered with ads for underarm deodorant, the connection being, obviously, that secret agents sweat a lot. Kleenex produced video segments of real people talking about life and, not surprisingly, crying. Other examples range from BMW's groundbreaking series of Internet-only mini-movies, featuring hot directors like *Brokeback Mountain*'s Ang Lee, to Starbucks' hosting songs on iTunes, and Budweiser's radical announcement in early 2007 of bud.tv, a website conceived as an entertainment channel featuring original programs, but only if you took the time to register first.[6] It didn't fare too well, by the way.

   Nowhere in any of this do we see overt messages like "buy our paper clips, or drink our beer," but instead consumers are expected to sense the association between the content of the programming and the brands. Forget relevance to behavior. This isn't anything other than branding as pleasant distraction.

Corporate-created content is
mostly branding by osmosis.

2. **Branding as mash-up tool.** Super Bowl XLI was notable not so much for the entertaining ads, but for being the first game to have viral components built into it. This was branding designed to be reused first, and understood or internalized some time thereafter. For instance, one spot featured people greeting one another with a slap to the face. It didn't really work as a commercial per se, as it certainly had no connection with a reason to drink or eat or buy whatever it was advertising. But it was tailor-made to get converted into a computer file, reassembled into different combinations, and then posted and forwarded online.

Most branding mash-up isn't so organized. There's a thriving world of edits and adaptations swapped and viewed on the Internet: some are funny, lots are gross, and all of them carry a patina of credibility because people are creating them for a purpose other than selling something. There's no way to direct or control it, as GM discovered when its early campaign to elicit consumer-generated mash-ups of its Tahoe SUV footage resulted in some angry and anti–gas guzzler results.[7]

Branding, which was once an activity so complex and esoteric that you needed a degree to do it, is now the purview of *American Idol* popularity contests. Anybody can do it. Blogging is mash-up. Companies input comments into a chat, and people edit by adapting, commenting, and otherwise changing it.

So these two corporate strategies—corporate-created content and mash-up—are intended to make us all consumer/producer *owners* of branding.

In the last chapter, we saw that search behavior is a new key driver of consumer purchase intent. To respond to that with corporate or user-created content is a misread of the situation, and a misuse of advertising and marketing money. Worse, even if the Myth of the Consumer/Producer were a relevant idea, behavioral reality still makes it *just not true*.

CONTEXT AND REPETITION

Underneath all of the hopeful rhetoric of branding and the Myth of the Consumer/Producer exists the reality of, well, reality.

Nobody is asking for more branding.

Imagine you were standing on an empty street corner and yelling at people as they walked by on their way to a sporting event. You could scream loud enough to overpower most conversations as people passed, and literally demand their attention. Eventually, passersby would catch on and start avoiding you by walking on the other side of the street, or taking new ways to the stadium. So you'd move your rant to the sporting event itself, and set up your act on a seat in the grandstand. There, you might find yourself surrounded by thousands of other people just like you, each with his or her own loud screed. So you'd yell louder, maybe dance around or gesture wildly. So would they. You'd see them; they'd see you. And the sporting event would go on.

Presence is not the same as *recognition*. It's common knowledge that people no longer want to view commercials. They don't possess the time to do so, nor they are able or willing to retain or use the marketing messages contained therein. One study suggests that two-thirds of people would like to skip or block marketing entirely, and over half avoid buying products that overwhelm them with commercials.[8] It's almost as if consumers are *running away from branding altogether*, and marketers are chasing them, increasing the average consumer's exposure to marketing messages to over a million per year (versus as little as one-fifth of that in the 1970s).[9]

The Myth of the Consumer/Producer says that the answer to this crisis is to deliver *more* programming with *less* useful purposes.

Yet the reality of consumer behavior renders the myth powerless to effect any real change in your branding results:

- **First,** the "half-life" of viral branding is in inverse proportion to its immediate impact. If marketers can successfully achieve some recognition for a logo, or something blowing up or shockingly strange, the segments people will see most will be viewed over the shortest period of time. That makes sense, in that the catchiest content gets circulated the fastest. User-created content, like a virus, doesn't survive for long. The best stuff, that is seen most widely, is also seen most briefly.

- **Second,** viewing viral video is truly like catching a cold; the experience is characterized more by symptoms than by root causes. When someone has a head cold, the evil machinations of viruses aren't describable, but the symptoms certainly are (runny nose, itchy eyes, and plugged ears). The content that the consumer/producer uses or forwards is similarly symptomatic: Nobody remixes brand messages or forwards video footage because it says something meaningful about a company. Imagine getting that e-mail link titled "Look at How Joy Dishwashing Liquid Has Upped Its Surfactant Quotient!" Corporate messages are edited, parsed, dissected, and recast. Entertainment content is enjoyed. End of story.

- **Third,** democracy is a great leveler of all things, including branding. At some point, the videos and blogs, mash-up footage, and all the Internet shorts start to look the same. No branding can hope to own boobs, buffoonery, or blather. So what branding benefit was achieved by the footage of slapping mentioned earlier? Presume that every living human being saw it, along with the edits and knockoffs that followed. Anyone could film and e-mail it, and chances are somebody in a basement somewhere did it one slap better. The Burger King mascot posed with swimsuit models in 2006, so the next few hundred similar clips had much less impact, if any at all. In this sense, making my own cut-up video for my beverage client was no different than me making one about my dog.

- **Fourth,** there's the issue of *escalation*. As the content gets more and more similar, *it becomes less interesting*, prompting the creators to either make the stuff more shocking or risk losing viability in the marketplace. I know this observation is nothing new. There's a good chance that old men in tights and flowered hats sat around in Renaissance Italy and bemoaned the coarsening of popular culture. It's a truism that whatever was shocking last year is commonplace now, and next year will yield something worse. Since the language of images, sounds, and themes available to the consumer/producer is fairly limited, the only way to overcome this inevitable trend is to get louder, stranger, or angrier. So the branding that was irrelevant to your business this year has to get crazier and less relevant in order to be seen next year.

- **Fifth,** at some point the consumer/producer simply bows out of the game, doesn't she? The seventh time a friend innocuously recommends a product to you is nowhere near as believable as the third time. Checking your favorite video website for the dumbest footage just isn't as superbly and entertainingly worthwhile as it once was. A blogger voicing his opinion on another very personal experience and declaring it to be a universal truth comes across as not really so universal after all.

You've likely experienced this aspect of the consumer/producer phenomenon if you ever got on one of those joke e-mail distribution lists: you clicked on the first handful of jokes when they made the rounds the first few times. But I'd bet money that you don't do it so much anymore.

So are we all really becoming consumer/producers, and if so, are we really interested in consuming and producing *branding*?

The content most people make is brief, blatantly exploitative, boorish, and oftentimes just plain bad.

Ultimately, since presence in this context isn't synonymous with recognition, and recognition seems ever more distanced from real sales or business benefit, your judgment as a businessperson would tell you that this might not be the right environment in which to *give up ownership of the brand*, or to expect from it anything that helps your business. Wasting consumers' time is a behavior that is ultimately worthless, or perhaps worse. You just know that selling isn't generated or supported this way.

The user-created content approach to branding is the equivalent of a communications drive-by shooting.

Proponents of the myth will counter that that media are *channels* through which only memorable messages can stand out amidst an increasing cacophony of other messages. Beyond the viral/buzz phenomena, this traditional belief applies to a sponsor segment on *The Milton Berle Show* just as it's true for an SMS voting promotion for that top models show. *The only change is that the threshold for awareness is higher*, because there's so much more to vote, comment, or crap upon.

But most consumer consumption of media is not experienced

via one-way channels anymore, but rather as an aspect of the two-way *places* in which consumers live and function. They're busy replying, editing, changing, and doing lots of other things at the same time. Consumers are constantly in motion, swimming or floating aimlessly in a sea of other influences, activities, inputs, outputs, and whatever else occupies their scattered attention spans. Almost every media experience we have, from buying collectible spoons on eBay and slaughtering trolls in *World of Warcraft* to talking on our mobile phones, is a participatory, interactive experience within a rich context of simultaneous experiences. No amount of irreverence, shock, or sleaze is going to change this. A larger logo or ad before I can get to a website will not make a difference.

What consumers retain is inversely related to how much they touch and do.

I can imagine that you've heard from your friendly local neighborhood branding guru (or the last book on your nightstand) something like this: "Branding is all about ubiquity, and repeating the brand messaging via numerous touchpoints delivers awareness and retention of the positioning." Maybe you've heard this as the reason why your company should fund another year of branding, or perhaps it has been used in connection with explaining a specific campaign that has shown no perceivable impact whatsoever on your business. Perhaps you've said something like this to your boss, or to a client. The reality of how consumers behave suggests you might want to request a bit more thoughtful analysis before you write the next check, or pitch the next campaign.

Propagation of useless, irrelevant content is useless and irrelevant.

Imagine a photo spread on your favorite photo sharing site, maybe of a guy balancing a jar of peanut butter on his nose. The myth qualifies any visits to this collection as branding. We have to accept the premise that even a casual encounter with imagery (or any content) results in awareness and retention.

Further, it's common knowledge that when you want to remember something, like a phone number or somebody's name, you repeat it a few times. Same goes for branding. Simply counting visits and/or "eyeballs" has intrinsic value, even if we can't directly connect them to any sales effect. Branding educates people. It primes the marketplace, "out there" somewhere. Repetition yields adoption, and adoption influences behavior.

Unfortunately, connecting the guy's balancing act to some eventual purchase decision to buy peanut butter requires a suspension of disbelief that would also allow us to converse with fairies and gnomes. We human beings just don't operate on the same wavelength as all of this creative garbage.

Our psyches are less unbounded cosmoses of thoughts and more like ordered shopping lists. As one leading neuroscientist explains, choices are thrust upon every waking moment of every living thing, whether we're human beings or squirrels. Options have to be evaluated in real time, costs and benefits weighed, and then decisions made to move on to the next choice.[10]

We incorporate our direct experience into this constantly updated list; then we both consciously and unconsciously reorder it, based on mood, circumstances, and opportunity. It's a wholly subjective and fluid feedback loop. It's also a filter. Our past experiences affect what we choose to contemplate, how we consider it, and the conclusions we derive therefrom. Nothing is concrete or unchanging. Our brains are marvelous machines that, quite literally, re-create reality moment to moment.

When a branding image pops up like a billboard on an instant messaging chat window, the consumer has the split-second moment to reorder experience and knowledge. Dumb commercial repeated three times while I'm watching a football game on TV? It's still dumb the third time I see it, only I learn to get up and fix my sandwich. If I didn't click the web page banner ad the first time I saw it, I won't do so the twelfth time. Attention is reallocated in real time, and consumers' focus moves accordingly. If branding doesn't contain information relevant to my behavior at the moment I experience it, it's unlikely that I'm going to file it away somewhere in my subconscious or use it in any meaningful way later on.

People make choices based on a running list of priorities.

It's funny that consumers live in such a moving, behavioral-driven reality, yet the language marketers use to talk about brands is static and thought-dependent:

- **Positioning.** As if brands set something in stone.
- **Frame of reference.** Presuming that marketers can set dimensions for thinking, like a border around a painting or TV screen.
- **Point of difference.** Like a snapshot of prioritization, assuming that what matters for consumers one moment will be identical to the next.

- **Barrier to competitive entry.** As if marketers can create a way to stop consumers from considering alternatives.

- **Touchpoints.** As if consumers are reaching out for brands instead of real products and services, or that a company can channel where and how people will learn about them.

CONTENT IS *NOT* KING

Few phrases get used as often in the creative world as "content is king." It is a direct homage to the primacy of meaning in our lives, and a reference to the importance of what people put *into* art versus how, when, or where they get anything *out of it*. It's also a presumption that artistic endeavors have an intrinsic value that supersedes any externality. Branding is based on it, whether today or fifty years ago.

But people don't consume things independent of place, time, and other variables. Content is inexorably infused with immediacy, and suffused with references to the *here and now* of experience. Every memory you possess has associated with it details of place, time, mood, odor, temperature, or any number of other qualities that your brain elected to note. That's why a branding message painted on a billboard doesn't work the same way as the same one in a magazine ad. An Internet offer run on a banner is useless if printed on a physical banner trailing an airplane overhead. The magazine ad has a different impact when read sitting in a doctor's office than when read on a treadmill, and the message trailing the plane is less effective if fewer people are on the beach. Time of day matters. So does weather. What was just read or experienced before encountering the ad has an effect, as does whatever else the person is doing while experiencing it, and what's coming thereafter.

So let's say a consumer is killing time looking at stupid videos or chatting with friends, and up comes some corporate-created content. Eyes glaze over the logo on the way to the play button. Favorite blogs are read, SMS messages received, comments made in chat rooms appear rapid-fire, one after the other. Content that's *most somethingorother* gets attention first, but experience is never independent of whatever else is going on at that moment. What is compelling one time is irritatingly petty the next. A video that didn't seem funny enough to forward one morning is a must-see for your friends if tripped over late at night.

Of course, there are always exceptions, but a general rule is that recognition and retention don't reside in the eyes of the beholder as much as *emerge from the qualities of the moment*. Ad agencies take circumstance into consideration, but usually apply it to how an ad will read or look, not in deference to the context of user experience. If anything, branding is intended to prompt consumer experience of more branding.

It's gloriously and madly circular logic, isn't it?

What's a brand promise if all it promises to do is waste your time?

Think again about standing on the corner and yelling at people as they pass by. Rainy day, nice day, low voice, shrill voice. One passerby versus the next. Same content, yet each experience is different.

The Myth of the Consumer/Producer relies on a fundamental quality of goodwill, or gullibility, that consumers will pay attention to something at least once, maybe twice. It's true that we can learn to link to a name or slogan if reminded, or consider a new bit of information or content in relation to something we already know. People also tend to look up reflexively when they hear a loud noise. We all clicked on the first few pop-up ads that appeared on our computer screens, or gave our e-mail and other contact details to the first companies that asked us to register online. Human begins are inherently trusting, as if we possess a genetic trust bank account for expenditure on experience. You've seen it with little kids who gleefully walk into crowds, or reach for an open flame. Or when you believe someone the first time they make a promise.

People maintain that trust bank account when it comes to the products and services they buy, too. We'll entertain communications for a bit, until we know better, as our ranking and prioritizing of what we care about and remember gets smarter. The *right* content on the *wrong* day, or content somehow mismatched to the environment of the moment, and the branding spends down the account instead of building it up.

I'd offer that most of the branding content consumers experience today doesn't *build* brand equity, but rather *spends* it, like a debit card. Prioritization doesn't allow for a category of *to-be-decided* elements in consumers' minds, whether conscious or not. They need to move on to the next choice. People don't just endure branding; they use it and discard it. For every branding experience that doesn't have an immediate, meaningful impact on our lives, there is a deduction. Our accounts are always current.

Behavior, not content, is king.

Yet every newfangled branding activity that uses purposeless creative content to prompt those rare, costly moments when consumers will actually pay attention . . . gives them purposeless branding content. It's like raising your hand in class for months and never being called on, then when you finally get the chance to speak, you forget what it was you wanted to say. Or you buy a lottery ticket for years, and then forget the number when the winning card is drawn.

This is the miraculous feedback-loop quality of the Myth of the Consumer/Producer: Marketers have these brief moments to interact with consumers, and they use them to get the consumers to interact with branding, instead of giving them something relevant to the moment and to their Chronologies of Purchase Intent. *Marketers are still thinking about thinking,* instead of prompting a subsequent behavior that would be more valuable than a chuckle or gasp.

Branding can't be about capturing share of mind if it hopes to be relevant to your business. It must capture *share of moment.*

Portion of life.

Consumer/producers don't necessarily want to absorb branding, and they don't want to create more of it. They want it to contribute to their lives and contribute back to the lives of others. That means providing actionable things that are relevant to them, not reflecting back to some abstraction of brand. Successful branding has nothing to do with what people think about branding, but rather what they do with it in real behaviors. And the farther that *doing* is from making a purchase, the more likely the branding cost is truly an expense that both company and consumer will pay for, and get little to nothing in return.

When was the last time anybody involved in branding in your organization had a conversation about *context* and *behavior*? If you're in the branding business, how have these components factored into your planning? You might want to obliquely suggest conversation that explores the implications of two basic facts:

1. The Myth of the Consumer/Producer encourages the delivery of branding that is no more relevant to the business goals of the company than traditional branding.

2. Expending a rare, costly interaction with consumers on some abstraction of brand—however strategic or entertaining it might be—misses an opportunity to influence behavior.

Branding without behavior—as the trigger for retention in memory, and/or as a call to action within or upon experience—

is an expense with no payback beyond self-congratulation. This truth becomes ever more apparent when we see branding in service of the Myth of the Consumer/Producer.

The virtual construct of images and symbols that used to comprise the content of brands is no more relevant when people can manipulate them. In fact, without even the slightest hint of relevance to subsequent consumer behavior, one could argue that the content is rendered not only less effective, but actively damaging to your business. You can't afford to have what little time your consumers might spend contemplating anything involving your business focused on something that doesn't motivate them.

Entertaining consumers does wonders for the quality of life on our planet, but will do little for your sales.

Already, there are innovative companies that are exploring ways to prompt behaviors that are meaningful to their businesses. IBM invested $100 million in the first quarter of 2006 for a two-year campaign to communicate with 53,000 employees, their families and friends, clients, and vendors. The program, a new business idea generator called InnovationJam, may not have been conceived as branding per se, but it was quite possibly the smartest investment IBM has made in its brand for years. Here's why:

- **It was targeted.** One of the conceits of the Myth of the Consumer/Producer is that viral messages can and should be transmitted to strangers, and then passed to other strangers. This makes most viral marketing a *glorified chain letter*. The IBM program activated people who have a vested interest in IBM's success—folks who function as parts of the company's "genome"—so they're more willing to hear the messaging, more hopeful that it is successful, and more likely to share it with their own imprimatur.

- **It was actionable.** The InnovationJam campaign didn't tell people what to think, it got them to think things as a natural outcome of doing something. Consider the many millions of dollars IBM and its competitors spend to broadcast all that interchangeably expansive and inert brand advertising in print and on Sunday morning public affairs TV. Whether it was telling people to "think different," "go somewhere," or ponder their own navel lint, there's really no call to action in any of it. So my guess is that most people don't really pay much attention to it.

- **It was self-sustaining.** The program minted its own branding dollars by spinning off any number of additional programs. Blogs picked them up and talked about them, sharing ideas and what-ifs. Groups of would-be innovators pooled their resources and time, like glorified team lottery ticket purchasers.

What IBM got with the InnovationJam is branding that is truly integrated with the function of the company. It got people to *do things*, and thus it reached beyond the attention IBM itself could ever have purchased directly. Its activities provided any number of ways to measure the return on investment, and to prompt continued dialogue with people that might lead to purchase.

Unfortunately, most of the latest branding is not so useful. Most *new* media ideas are revised versions of *old* media ideas. The tactics change, but the deliverables don't. Branding remains all about creating, perpetuating, and banking upon a sexy myth. The Myth of the Consumer/Producer is just the latest iteration. It won't be the last.

Our approach to the challenge of the marketplace is still hobbled by our old ideas about brands, as if the results of our preconceptions were an eight-hundred-pound gorilla in the room that we really can't allow ourselves to see. No Myth of the Consumer/Producer is going to let us avoid the truth for long. Budgets will fray. Expectations will rise. Marketing industry meetings will celebrate the latest silver-bullet technology solutions. Yet some time soon, business needs will demand we face the real issue: we need to stop talking an *it* of brands, or that it matters.

The only real proof for your brand is *behavior*, and in this realization is the empowerment to create new experiences, new benefits, and new competitive tools for your business. You'll see how this approach starts to unfold in respect to social media, which we'll explore in the next chapter.

But first I need to go watch a few inane videos. Just kidding.
Sort of.

The Outsourcing of Consent

I spend one weekend every year with baseball fanatics.

The Baseball Buddies Caravan is a loose group of guys who go to spring training preseason baseball games, alternating our gatherings between Florida and Arizona. Truth be told, I'm the interloper in the club. I enjoy going to games for the experience of sitting in the stands, eating junk food, and otherwise spending a chunk of hours not clicking away at my keyboard. In this way, I resemble many of the loyalists of other national pastimes, such as an average cricket fan in the UK, or one of many Canadians whose run-of-the-mill interest in hockey or curling surpasses awareness but stops somewhere just north of tolerance.

I like it that we form a *community* that possesses a context far richer than that which baseball provides: the game weekends are simply a touchpoint for a scope of engagement that ranges across the totality of our lives. My friends influence my decisions, and I have influenced theirs, from recommendations on music and movies to thoughts about parenting and politics. We celebrate births and mourn deaths. It's as if, when we talk about baseball, we can't help but talk also about broader, bigger themes that are relevant to us.

Our gathering is a virtual *neighborhood* in which we live, which we reaffirm geographically once a year, but experience all year long. In fact, our neighborhood is far more real than many of the ersatz neighborhoods that real estate developers promote. Our physical presence at baseball games might be measured in hours, but our *citizenship* extends across 365 days.

People have been forming groups based on shared or complementary interests since the Sumerians started writing down their recipes for beer. Guilds, associations of artisans, clubs, team sports, political parties, religious congregations, environmental groups, animal shelters, and cooking clubs are all examples of people aggregating because of shared interests. Newscasters reference generic "communities" that have imagined consensus opinions or reactions to events, though it's mostly a rhetorical trick for presenting their own questions. Collections of individuals with a single shared interest are common: geeky rocket builders might get together simply to explode things, while grandmothers share sewing patterns.

Yet calling many of these aggregations of people "communities" is like calling two people with the same color eyes one, too.

I bet you've heard talk in your company about community, haven't you? You've likely gotten a presentation from an agency, or a mandate from a manager who has recently read something in a magazine on the brave new world of online communities. These communities are comprised of your customers, would-be customers, some subset of the most vocally happy, or groupings that are consistently critical. Or there are communities of people who have never bought your products at all and, for all you know, never will, but who have something to say about something you do (or failed to do). The rationale rationalizes that the people are there—*wher*ever and *when*ever there is—so your branding needs to be, too. Not to get too cute, but the *there* of these communities is also *here*, in that the phenomenon defies any effort to limit, control, or avoid these collections of friends, critics, customers, or space aliens. The business media are fascinated by it, celebrating companies that use tools like blogs, forums, and chat to blur the distinctions between company and customer, all in the service of a philosophy of "radical transparency."[1]

If you believe the hype, it's as if the existence of such groupings is a new phenomenon. The teenagers and twentysomethings who participate in online conversation communities of any sort, also known as *social media*, represent a new species of human being, let alone consumers. To understand them, all you have to do is drag the nearest twentysomething into the next brand strategy meeting, get her opinion on what communities are hot with her contemporaries, and put your advertising there (or get your CEO to blog). There are new rules for branding, the overriding principle being that you need to *give up your brand* to this new channel. You *have* to spend money on it.

Well, no you don't. Since your brand doesn't really exist anywhere, there's nothing to "give up." But you also don't need to waste your time and money pretending otherwise.

When we're talking about people online, whether they're consumers or anonymous aggregations of folks, can the term "community" be applied and used effectively? Is this *conversation* with and within social media meaningful to your business, and if so, what should you do about it? Oh, and by the way, they're not just teenagers using the stuff.

There are endless books, articles, and new business pitches that will argue for you to shift your current old media branding expenditure (which you can't measure) to new, social media branding expenditures (that likewise defy accountability). *Have budget, will blog.* But if we cut through the chatter about the magical qualities of this phenomenon, which are promoted mostly by communications experts who want to sell it—or their boosters in the media, who hope to make money, too—I'd suggest that the solution-agnostic answers you will discover would be a solid *maybe* and a situational *it depends*.

Here are the three observations we need to consider:

1. When it comes to communities and conversation, whether online or off, most aren't communities, and few truly converse.

2. You need to understand the dynamics of what people do because of social media (truly new idea: *behavior*) versus what they say in and about it (really old idea: *perception*).

3. Whatever you subsequently do should deliver measurable and profitable benefits to your business.

Can you afford to ignore what's going on? No. Is social media the grand salvation of branding? Nope. Should you spend money experimenting without a clear understanding of the context? *Naw.*

Let's first spend a little time at a ball game together, and explore player behavior.

NOWHERE COMMUNITIES OF NOBODIES

Social media and social software/technology are often loosely defined as the same thing, namely being *communication tools that are computer-mediated and enable people to connect or collaborate.*

The universe of social media seems almost incomprehensibly diverse, ranging from multizillion-dollar aggregators of content and large, corporate-owned productions to the small, crazy person in his basement—run blog that can claim only the guy who writes it as a dedicated reader.

There are any number of analyses that categorize these media with the nuanced subtlety of rating fine wines, along with all of the nonsense of Y2K-like labels and acronyms. One advertising agency classifies twenty-five different flavors of blog.[2] You've likely sent instant messages, texted on your mobile phone, commented in a forum on an Internet site, maybe posted a fix to a product website, and regularly read blogs or write your own. The list changes almost daily, and you see the latest and greatest at www.baskinbrand.com.

Maybe you've used Craigslist or Angieslist to find a used bicycle, TripAdvisor to find a hotel room, Yelp to locate a restaurant, or Match to find a date. There is no shortage of invention in this category, as connecting people who want or need to do something with each other just screams *moneymaking opportunity* to venture capitalists and financiers, who fund these services as often as people buy their morning coffee. Maybe a name I've mentioned is already defunct, or two others have emerged (or two dozen, or two hundred).

But forget about the buzz, and let's ask, "What happens in a real community?"

We have a couple of millennia of human history on this subject, along with recent behavioral studies that look at online behavior going back into the last century.[3] There are at least six core qualities:

1. **Transparency.** People need to possess known and knowable identities in order to participate. Anonymity allows for people to take extreme opinions on blog comments and in chat rooms. Detaching identity from behavior yields the basest, lowest-common-denominator online exchanges between anonymous characters registering statements, one after the other, and is not a conversation. So, for instance, you can't just post a flamer comment on my blog, Dim Bulb, but instead must be willing to identify yourself via prior registration. This doesn't really do much, though, as anyone can register as anyone else, so transparency is a rare commodity in social media.

2. **Authenticity.** No community allows members to take something without giving in return. Shared responsibilities and trust give

a community meaning, and require an investment of time or effort other than that required for entertainment. *Things matter* to the members of a community, not just because a word or punctuation mark pisses someone off. Citizens actually *converse* upon occasion. I can't get my band rated on garageband .com until I rate fifteen others first, for instance.

3. **Interactivity.** Not only do they converse, but neighbors do so in as many unconscious and/or unplanned ways as they do by schedule or intent. For all of their shared issues and concerns, they define *living* in terms that are much more mundane and real-time. Interactivity isn't just elective. Out of impromptu exchanges can come some of the best rewards of true conversation within a community.

4. **Virtuality.** It's been said that there is no Japan per se, but rather just Japanese people, who carry what defines *Japan-ness* with them wherever they go in the world. Communities are active within individuals even when those individuals are not actively in the communities. You don't just log in, nor is your community limited to one place or time.

5. **Applicability.** An extension of virtuality is that communities aren't just integrated into individuals' psyches, but also yield information or behaviors that occur in real life. I take things I experience in one community and apply them to other ones. Another way of looking at this is that, because of the requirement of depth of involvement, real communities overlap and are often integrated.

6. **Sustainability.** A real community has a reason to exist over time. So a fad isn't a community, nor is a rage, flashmob, collection of disgruntled customers, or passing topic of news interest. Usually, this existence relates to many of the other qualities of community, in that there are reasons people get and stay truly

involved. There's an accepted or collective wisdom to communities. A community has a point of view (or views).

Do any of the latest or most popular social media tools you've heard about exhibit all, or even a majority, of the qualities of real communities? Upon reflection, I wonder if my baseball friends and I even qualify.

The vast majority of communities online aren't really communities at all, but rather various permutations of directories, repositories, bulletin boards, or lists. Many don't come close to exhibiting the shared sensibilities that arise—in virtual or real life—among travelers waiting at an airport taxicab queue, the communities of magazine subscribers, or even the purposes evident among members of a gym. There are certainly groupings of people who are grouped for a reason, but it rarely amounts to more than the happenstance of shared, fleeting purpose. Virtual reality looks a hell of a lot like *real* reality, it turns out.

It's no surprise that while we marketers talk about social media, we look at most online communities as glorified *channels* for delivering advertising. The *socialness* is just the latest trick to attract viewers for your branding messages. Our broad, imprecise definition of community leads us to look at the *who* of these so-called communities, instead of the *what* they're hoping to do.

So branding strategy continues unchanged from a generation ago, focused on psychographic *what-if*, instead of behavioral *so-then*. This has made it possible to tee up social media as the potential salvation for placing the ads (or words in conversation) that used to go into television and print. It's where we find those mythical consumer/producers of the last chapter. And for a dumb idea, this approach has generated oodles of profits.

Then again, branding still makes billions for traditional media, too.

Both approaches rely on delivering to advertisers the same broad demographic groupings that are supposed to care about branding. And since these expenditures are apart from expenditures with causal links to sales, the approaches stay in use.

GM's Pontiac division shifted its entire ad budget online for the launch of the G5 a few years ago: Internet ads, a showroom in virtual world Second Life, a page and promotion on MySpace, and blog entries were celebrated as bold because, by the very nature of where the stuff was placed, the company had thus targeted young, hip people.[4]

The Pontiac marketers deserve credit for their experiment, but the *content* of the branding itself smacked of the same old ideas and behavioral disconnects that could have been placed as bookends on broadcast television shows, arranged in glossy magazine ads, or promoted on local AM news radio. Participants in the MySpace campaign had to *buy a car* before they could participate in the "Friends with Benefits" program, when most everything else they could do online costs absolutely *zilch*. I'd wager that few teenagers trolling the site for e-mails from friends were terribly interested in cars during that activity anyway, however closely they might have fit the imagined demographic of entry-level car purchasers. Ultimately, the Pontiac campaign was no more contextually meaningful than getting a telemarketer call at home during dinner. It was envisioned to appeal to the *who* of the visitors, versus the *what* of their visits.

People visit these so-called communities with even less focused attention than they ever gave to commercials on TV or ads in magazines. No wonder this medium comes cheaper than the older, analog media. GM touted the fact that it could shave lots of cash from its marketing budget by shifting its ads online. Such pricing must reflect the fact that it's even easier for consumers to ignore a banner ad than it is to hang up the phone when that telemarketer calls. Perhaps the free market is efficient after all.

Most online communities are not communities, but rather **places** where people go to do something.

The old channel approach is not the answer for your new media branding experiments. In fact, it's doomed, because social media are not channels, but rather *places* where people go to do things. Throwing useless entertainment at them is pointless, and hoping to attach a brand name to a generic emotion is at best wishful thinking. While we'll explore more about what real online communities might accomplish for your business, we need first to explore in more detail the idea of *conversation*.

TALK ISN'T JUST CHEAP, IT'S OFTEN WORTHLESS

On March 11, 2007, Alexander Wolfe published a blog post on InformationWeek.com entitled "A Band About Nothing: Remembering Boston's Brad Delp," in which he pondered the meaning of the recent demise of the band's lead singer. What followed was a litany of reader posts that were accusations, diatribes, obscenities, and even a few threats. Postings on product-related articles on the site received similar results (a piece on the likelihood of Apple's success with the iPhone met with angry statements, with liberal use of words like "idiot" and "stupid").

Wolfe, a senior editor at *InformationWeek*, explained the phenomenon to me: "One warning sign for marketers to watch out for is that, when reader posts start to run amok, what may be happening is that you *think* you're having a conversation with your customers, but you're really having a *versation* . . . they're proceeding with comments independent of others, and aren't really interacting at all. We experienced this firsthand when a podcast of ours generated so many hits that the servers crashed, so only the first few visits got to the audio. But that didn't stop people from commenting on it. Comments followed other comments, irrespective of whether they'd actually heard the podcast or not. People weren't *listening*. They just wanted to be *heard*."

Many corporate sites don't fare much better. Soon after its inception, Dell's ideastorm.com had a posting begging for a moderator, which prompted over a hundred responses over the next month, few of which built on the last post, or affected what followed (it has since evolved). Special-interest sites and blogs often feature comments that are barely a loose approximation of dialogue. What nominally passes for a conversation is usually a string of declarative statements, one after the other, intended less to share information or to persuade, and more to establish or affirm an individual position or presumed reputation.

Have blog will announce, the theory might go. Online conversation enables a "Me Decade," only anonymized and electrified, allowing for a flourishing of self-interested expression far beyond anything a hippie or EST-addicted disco dude could have ever imagined. You'd likely hear better and more thoughtful dialogue were you to eavesdrop on two five-year-olds discussing ownership of a toy.

Businesses have been dealing with disgruntled or otherwise outspoken customers since the first monk complained that his quill malfunctioned. The traditional equation has been that the loudest or most difficult customers often were the least profitable, so the strategy was often to minimize their interaction (or encourage them to stop being customers altogether).

Much of what goes on online is just plain irrelevant to your business.

A litany of statements online, even if it approximates a real give-and-take dialogue, has no more intrinsic worth than a chat between two people standing at a bus stop outside your office building. Someone creating a home video of your product getting smashed with a hammer, and then eliciting online comments about how stupid he is, has no more value than if he'd done it purely for the edification of his adoring family. Chat about something right or wrong about your business is usually inconsequential talk, irrespective of where it occurs. Not every problem is worth a response, and many don't warrant acknowledgment. "Radical transparency" is a catchphrase, nothing more.

For each conversation that experts will tell you matters because it leads to other conversations, a hundred give-and-takes mean absolutely nothing. Whatever self-perpetuating cycle that might result is still mostly talk. Words. An *implicit potentiality*, if it's a potential at all. Brand remains a state of mind, like always, only now the mind is a hive, and its synapses buzz with every blogger keystroke.

There is much to be learned and done here, but approaching social media as just another tool to influence what people *think* seems to miss the boat, or leave out the potentially largest benefit. The point of conversation—*any conversation*—can't be simply to converse, whether online, via older, one-way branding, or over the roar of the jets with your plane seatmate. Talk can be entertaining, but alone it rarely is enough to make money for anybody, unless you're a stand-up comedian.

Conversation without behavior is just more talk.

MEET MY ID (AND ALL HIS FRIENDS)

"You don't necessarily want to try selling real-world lingerie to the scantily clad woman in Second Life, because the person behind that avatar could very well be a guy," explained Greg Verdino, a marketing executive with one of the best new-media blogs in the business.[5] "To be sure, there's always a real person behind the avatar and that real person could very well turn into a loyal customer—but with a virtual world like Second Life it's nearly impossible to tell exactly who you're dealing with and even harder to draw a clear conclusion about how even the richest virtual engagement might translate into real-world results. In other words, selling them virtual products, or expending their virtual time, isn't the same thing as selling them products in the real world."

Greg recapped the experience of a shoe company, in which its agency was able to determine that the client's average consumer spent approximately six aggregate minutes "engaged with the brand" through traditional mass media channels over the course of an entire year, but that a social media launch had gotten users to spend twice that much time. Thousands of virtual sneakers were sold for pennies apiece. Yet how many real pairs of shoes did the client sell as a result? You can guess the answer. I wonder if it actually *hurt* real sales.

When one is looking to find connections to real-world behavior, the grassroots, single-subject nature of a large portion of the social mediascape is an interesting aspect to consider. If I love fly fishing, I can visit fishingjones.com or any of dozens of other weblogs dedicated to the minutiae of rods, hooks, and worms. My obsession with live hens can be satiated via the cams on hencam.com.

Even more interestingly, these grassroots tools intertwine with one another, just like the roots or grasses would do underground. So when I indulge my fascination with mechanical pencils by posting comments on davesmechanicalpencils.blogspot.com, I also get a listing of links to other related blogs that I can visit. There's a significant element of *discovery* to this media, which looks a lot like the discovery phase of the game model we'll look at in the next chapter.

Instead of focusing on the text that is supposed to approximate conversation in many of these supposed communities, consider how social media give each of us *the opportunity to realize our aspirational selves*. Maybe it's not about an "us" after all, but all about "me."

No longer do I have to be content with secreting my dream of being a judge on *American Idol* to idle contemplation; now I can tell people their singing is pitchy via any number of music ratings sites. If I'm feeling unempowered, I can go flame someone's chatroom posting. My baseball friends can realize their aspirations to be coaches and bless or curse player trades. Teenage girls can present themselves as bad-girl starlets on MySpace web pages, or as any number of other permutations of personality, on any number of websites. MMORPG (massive multiplayer online role-playing game) players are no longer wedded to their physical selves, but instead wield enormous swords, conjure magic, and live according to pseudo-medieval morality. Your friend named shoefanatic2009 on IM is obsessed with shoes, and nothing more. You may not even know if it's a he or a she, or if it's a real friend of yours in any sense of the term.

There is no single whole *you* online when you log on, but rather *a number of yous* experiencing things online in a number of different places, depending on the time, your mood, and what's currently available. This isn't dishonesty as much as a revelation of potential experience. I no longer have to satisfy my desire for power and authority that I would have once satisfied with buying a product. Now I can live out my aspiration via touting off on things via my blog, or dispensing technical advice to the huddled masses in product help forums. I don't need to buy membership in an exclusive club in my town when I can join one for free online. That black double-breasted suit I've always dreamed of wearing but couldn't because it would make me look four feet tall in the real world? I can talk in a chat room about how much I love wearing it, and there I'm six foot five inches, thank you very much. I have another avatar on another social site that's a floating chess piece.

___

We no longer need brands to express ourselves and our aspirations. Social media let us live those fantasies.

___

Branding was never simple or clear-cut, and now it's a whole lot more complicated. In fact, applying branding principles to conversations or interests of these online virtual selves is a daunting challenge. If people aren't just stopping off at a site to chat with a friend, they're letting some aspect of their selves search or troll around within a social media tool. Each aspect of a *self* possesses its own needs, rules, and requirements; every feeling, interest, and desire, freed from the fetters of propriety and accountability, is a difficult, ephemeral presence, rendered ever harder to quantify and corral by its very own incompleteness. A few online communities demand greater transparency and identification from their members, yet most travels through social media require (and provide) little to none.

Whether I am chatting, playing, helping, or buying, it's not me but my *ids* that are online.

So not only is it difficult to ponder how you might deliver branding to these presences that is relevant both to their activities and to the particular version of self they're exploring at that moment, but it prompts the question of *why* you'd ever want to do it at all. "They certainly don't want branding sent at them, at least not unless it's relevant to what they're doing at that precise moment," explained danah boyd, a social media researcher and blogger.[6] "This is seen as spam, and no one likes spam.

"That said, they are more than happy to consume advertisements because they see this as a fair trade for the free technology. They are interested in adverts or branding being pushed at them only when it's seen as extremely relevant, cool, and meaningful. For example, if Cool Brand X decides to direct-message a small minority of teens with an exclusive offer that will help them gain status amongst their peers, they'll pay attention. But if it's just another mass message with nothing more than an embedded advert, it's considered skeevy."

Establishing relevance to each of the aspects of my id is a dicey proposition, and it makes breaking through media clutter tougher than just being noticed or remembered at any cost. Yet much of what passes for social media online is the same stuff that was peddled a hundred years ago, only wrapped in a lot more highfalutin buzzwords. It's the penny press on steroids, when the cost of entry for any individual or group announcing to the world their heartfelt thoughts about, say, balls of rubber bands, or soap suds residue, is no more than the price of a computer and an Internet connection. The challenge isn't to find ways to participate in the resulting noise, but rather to find ways to make outcomes that are relevant to your business.

Conversation online is a means, not an end. And those ends define *community*, or the lack thereof.

SOCIAL, NOT TECHNICAL

The fundamental reason to use social media should be no different from any other tool on which your business spends money: it should help your company sell things, in tangible ways no different from the interest income your bank accounts accrue or the sheets of paper your staplers bind. Return on investment should be a measure, not a metaphor bent to implicitly allow conduct of activities that are explicitly pointless. Every new rule that requires the abandonment of an older principle—whether in recruiting, raw resources sourcing, or branding—is more than likely not going to be right (or all that new). If you need to ignore fundamentals of business and reporting to do it, it's a warning sign that it's quite possibly wrong.

Who cares if gazillions of people use your company icon, bits of video footage on their personal web pages or posted mash-ups, or talk about you incessantly? In this environment, your traditional branding communications have no more inherent meaning or relevance than the Bayeux Tapestry, or models of the element actinium. They're artifacts, or props, just like the declarations and obscenities many errant bloggers propagate into the cybervoid.

I know it sounds heretical, but approaching social media as if they're communities having conversations is wrong. They're *places* where, ideally, *people make decisions*. Everything leading up to it is just glorious branding foreplay.

As such, you should be more frightened than encouraged by many of the recent experiments that deliver ways to creatively waste consumers' time in service of brand. We've replaced the *interruption model* of advertising—hoping to insert stuff people don't want to see within things they do—with a *distraction model*. The idea that anybody would or want to "engage with your brand" is as old as branding itself, and is an inward-looking approach that elevates (or centralizes) the externality of brand as the point of interest for consumers, while focusing the communication strategy, content, and delivery at internalizing it within those individuals. It's a branding wet dream come true.

But it's backwards.

Social media show us that communication happens at the external, group level, *between* participants. They're engaged with each other, and the dynamic is peer-to-peer, not top-down from a corporate sponsor. If your communication is relevant, only then does anything seep down and into individual consumers with the potential for having benefits to business. While it might appear as though people are using social media to find content, don't be fooled. *Users are the content*, and they're not online to create branding, but to share, discuss, and draw conclusions. They're behaving online—living one of possibly numerous different personalities—and simply expressing themselves with images, icons, and grammatically abused acronyms. Don't confuse the messages with the medium.

"There are two phenomena going on here simultaneously," explained MIT's Henry Jenkins, one of the seminal thinkers on new media, business, and culture, "and they're two very different things. First, you have the wisdom of crowds, wherein anonymous people provide information independent of each other, a process that may yield—through aggregation—more accurate predictions than you could get from individual experts. Then you have collective intelligence, which is based on collaboration and deliberation, and involves people pooling information and refining their models over time. Both aspects of social media are impacting the shape and investment in brand."

The big kahuna of social media surfaces if and when people in real communities prompt behaviors that mean something to your business. That itself is not branding, nor is the conversation necessarily relevant, but the conclusions that enable actions are what matter: *affirmation, recommendations, help, authentication, consensus*, even *trust*. Social media have the potential to become the sounding board, echo chamber, and peer group for individuals to find support for their beliefs and intentions, as well as approval (or forgiveness) for their actions.

In such communities, people don't own your brand. *Their behaviors are your brand.*

This all-important, powerfully potent quality of social media is something I call *the outsourcing of consent*. Your branding can't make decisions for people, the community does. So what matters to them isn't what you say, but what consumers talk about; what questions they ask, not what you tell them; how they share, not how you confuse or distract them with your marketing. Social media are less conversation, and more mirror.

Consider this retail experiment: In 2007, Bloomingdale's started testing *social retailing* via an actual mirror that let shoppers send digital images of themselves trying on clothes to friends, who could then reply via IM with advice on whether to make the purchase or not. The clothes, the service, the store—all of it was part of a conversation *between* active consumers, not thrown at them or an engagement with some externality of brand. What were they conversing about? *Buying something.*

The business challenge is to recognize this behavior and figure out ways to enable it while not getting in its way.

The key understanding of social media is how and what consumers learn, and motivating them to do something.

Here's a nine-step cheat sheet for your next conversation about how to use social media:

Step 1. Determine the ecology of your social mediascape. Not all social sites are created equal, and you need to map them based on their hierarchy, dependencies, and the behaviors they prompt. There's a lot more going on here than just jumping into online chat rooms, or getting bloggers to mention your new product. Your analysis and ranking might take into account these attributes:

- **Voice.** Some social media, such as bloggers who follow technology (such as Lifehacker and Music-Tech-Policy), are a single/few writers talking, with others posting secondary comments.

Others, like Techguy, are open forums, where all voices are equal and pretty much run the show. Single talkers are more relevant to your plans (more focus, less blather).

- **Connectivity.** Bloggers tend to play favorites, and often comment and quote between one another. You can draw a flowchart of the most influential connections. Now extend it into the real world, and identify what social media elicit comments or provide info that appears in your employee suggestion box. What's the flow of online information that your sourcing team hears about from vendors on the telephone? You care more about social media that are connected, and less about those that exist in a virtual vacuum.

- **Behavior.** Some sites are purely entertainment (most of the video sharing tools, for instance). Others satisfy themselves with endless postings about infinitesimally minor or obscure aspects of your business. You don't care about the conversation as much as what behaviors come out of it. Do the social media make purchase recommendations? Solve problems? Review customer satisfaction? Prompt surveys, contests, or any other real-world actions?

- **Transparency.** This is a biggie. Social sites that allow visitors to participate anonymously are a lot less important that those that require name and/or some consistency of membership. You want to maximize your involvement with *whole* people, and minimize it with the *slivers* of personality that pose as anonymous trollers of single-interest sites.

- **Proximity.** Which media are truly independent, and which are somehow influenced or—gasp—controllable by your company? The origination of a social medium isn't anywhere as important as the credibility of its content.

So shouldn't you post pictures on Flickr or reply to comments on any reasonably active chat site, even if it doesn't fit into a plan and is practically free? No, because nothing is totally free (it costs you money and time), and everything you do fits into the ecology, so you live with the threat of unintended consequences if you do something that's not included in your plan. Want to post pictures? Figure out why it makes sense to do so. Want to talk? Go find a customer. Achieving conversation isn't a reasonable goal unless you can link it to something else.

Step 2: People interact with products and services, not brands. If you want the output from your social media involvement to be behaviors, your inputs need to be so, too. So every moment somebody spends interacting with your invented idea of brand is a moment wasted. What you want instead is for them to react to—or to anticipate and request—real behaviors that will prompt subsequent actions. It's this totality of interaction with your products and services that constitutes your brand, so look at your social media ecology and define:

- **What**. Some behaviors matter more than others, and your customers react to one issue more than another. Which are the clear *warning signs* that matter to you?

- **Where**. Identify where these behaviors originate. It's likely that most of the important influences on social media don't come from your branding or marketing groups.

- **How**. Do you want your target social media participants to act, other than think nice thoughts about your business? There are steps between awareness and purchase (remember the leaky sales funnel).

- **When**. Will those actions yield the relevance to your target social media participants (for each of those steps), and what is the likelihood that each will succeed?

Step 3: Think before and after product launches. Social media are a 24/7, ongoing reality, and, like any sales activity, the best time to ask for something is when you don't need it. So the last, worst time to engage in social media is when you launch a new product or service. Trying to control them then is like hitting your drum another time in hopes of changing the echo you've just heard.

Step 4: Social media programs don't start or end in marketing. The company behaviors that prompt consumer behaviors—and which are told and affirmed via social media—originate in customer service, new product research, vendor relations, human resources recruiting, employee communication, and any other function that involves one person recapping information gained from experience that impacts another, not just from propaganda.

The mirror that social media hold up to your business reflects every action, not just those words and images that you've decided constitute your brand. The ecology impacts whom you recruit, how long employees stay happily employed, whether vendors want to do business with you, and every other activity on which your business depends. It's these activities that may provide the influences on your product or services sales and, via those influences, prompt and guide the content of your presence in social media.

Step 5: What media *aren't* social? *American Idol* was just a poster child for the changes under way in television (the unreality of reality shows), but the definition of media—the ways in which people communicate—suggests that a number of different experiences in our lives could go from *involvement* to *participation*, whether formally considered "social" or not. Aren't most services that we use today moving toward an approximate functionality of social media? Start inserting other words, like "networks" or "services," and you see amazing potential for communities to emerge that are more real than most of what passes for it today:

- **Mobile phones.** By default, you have far more in common with your fellow service users than with most anonymous chatters you happen upon online. How long before these services are sold less on signal strength, and more on the social benefits of the community (wouldn't you trust restaurant reviews from a hundred people in your neighborhood versus opinions from anywhere else, for instance)?

- **Online auctions and services.** You're already a crowd-wisdom contributor when you buy a book at Amazon and then another visitor gets a recommendation, or you collectively collaborate when you post a favorite song list to your mp3 service. What if these services expanded—or new ones popped up—to aggregate and/or solicit recommendations? Think about Internet search for a minute, and your head explodes with possibilities (as we discussed in chapter 4).

- **Retail visits.** Couldn't bricks-and-mortar stores use every aspect of visit(s), from when consumers arrive and how long they stay, to where they go in the store and what they ultimately purchase, to then build social tools for fellow shoppers? Or use the tools to better configure the store and allocate products? Shopping is fundamentally a social function.

- **Loyalty programs.** Right now, I accrue frequent flyer/buyer/stayer/whatever points in a few dozen programs. Why isn't there more company-sponsored social connectivity within those programs? Tastes, desires, pricing, and lots of other things could be shared among fellow road warriors.

For your company, this means looking at most everything you do, whether buying TV ads or setting up a recruiting booth on a college campus, as a social media function. Call it whatever you want.

Step 6: Figure out how to stop conversations, not just start them. This smacks of shocking heresy, but the entire point of outsourced consent is to reach a conclusion that leads to action, right? So a conversation, however defined, is really a means to an end, the end being *behavior*, not *thought*. Prompt decisions, then. Challenge actions. Endeavor to migrate people out of the generic conversations and into ever closer dialogue with you.

Step 7: Once you realize that the conversation in most social media isn't really a conversation at all, it empowers you to do something you could never do in the real world: *just say no*. It's important that your hierarchy identifies all of the locations where you can afford to give minimal effort, if any. Anybody who promotes social media will tell you that you can't do this, and must talk to everyone who says something about your business. But it's just not true. A good number of people don't want to talk to you and you don't want to talk to them. Once you set priorities, stick to them.

Step 8: If you can't state a clear goal, don't do it. You can save oodles of money and get a better likelihood of success from the money you do spend if you have clear, business-compliant goals for your social media efforts.

Step 9: Build real communities. Start with your customers. Build a community up from the ground, basing it not on what you want to tell them, but what they need to get, give, and experience in order for you to achieve your sales goals. Every minute spent improving this concept of community is better spent than a minute doing battle with some anonymous naysayer cast adrift somewhere in the cybervoid.

Most analysts and thinkers agree that we're on the edge of an emerging phenomenon, and that some time soon there won't be just social programs and tools, but rather all of what we experience and do will have a link to someone or someplace else. Every nanosecond will be *searchable* and *communal*. In fiction, this is the moment when the robots rise up and try to terminate humanity. In pop culture, it's Terence McKenna's Timewave Zero, when novelty in the universe pings up to infinity. Both McKenna and the ancient Mayans agree that this'll occur sometime in 2012.[7]

Until then, however, we can talk about clicks and visits and eyeballs, and make lots of branding consultants rich. But the fundamental equation defining branding remains incomplete.

The last thing you need to do is spend more good money after bad. Understanding the behavior of groups and, upon occasion, real communities online, can help you develop a strategy to use them. Behavior matters more than words, so conversations matter when they yield actions.

The outsourcing of consent is a powerful idea that relies on a simple truism that you can put to work in your business tomorrow: conversation is useful because of what people do because of it (and, by direct result, what you get out of it).

So working in this medium can be useful, even if that means getting the occasional overload of baseball trivia along the way.

CHAPTER 7

Games as Purpose, Not Distraction

Anybody who talks about having a relationship with a brand has never been in love, had an addiction, or played a video game.

I got my first taste of video gaming as a teenager in the 1970s when, on a visit to the University of Illinois at Champaign-Urbana, I was shown a glowing orange computer screen on which a nascent online service called PLATO ran a game called *Empire*. A whopping thirty-two people could fight simultaneously in an intergalactic war that involved flying crude ships in configuration and typing commands that shot phasers at one another. The modems were about the size and speed of a straw stuck in a thick milkshake. Tracking ship movement sometimes required a dot-matrix printout of the screen coordinates so you could pause and plot your next move. But it was hard to remember to get up and take care of bodily functions, let alone eat or have a life. *Empire* wasn't a game; it was an addiction.

Perhaps the Egyptian pharaoh Reny-Seneb felt the same way about his board game *Dogs and Jackals* in 1800 B.C., since he chose to get buried with it. Gambling is just as compelling and just as old, as are its younger and more genteel cousins, hedge fund investing and writing insurance policies.

We're hardwired to play games, almost as if there is something that genetically predisposes us to feel rewarded by such interactive challenges. We've often said that hunters "play games" with their prey. Lovers do, too. When it comes to survival, we call what we do *work*; when it's simply for the fun of it, it's a *game*. Many of the experiential elements are the same, and when we interpret qualities of the latter as feedback from the former, we lead generally happier, if not more entertaining, lives.

Video games represent the latest, fastest-growing, and most engaging way to play. They range from low-involvement games like solitaire online, or *Snake* or *Tetris* on your mobile phone (these games are lumped into a category called "casual gaming"), to ever-higher-involvement games on portable game devices, freestanding consoles, computer MMORPGs (massive multiplayer online role-playing games, like *World of Warcraft*), and ARGs (alternate reality games, which combine virtual and real-world elements, pioneered by games like *The Beast* and *Majestic*).

This isn't some subculture phenomenon. What started in the days of *Empire* as primarily a geeky young guy thing has changed. Now 38 percent of all video-game players are women, and women older than eighteen represent a greater portion of the game-playing population (30 percent) than boys age seventeen or younger (23 percent).[1] Microsoft's online casual gaming site reported earlier this decade that over 65 percent of its 30 million registered users are women.[2] Nielsen Television Index has reported that 93.8 million people aged two or older averaged 135 minutes playing on an in-home game console, and all of them touched it at least once (representing a third of all TV households in the United States).[3] Korea leads the world in Internet usage and online gaming (MMORPGs).[4] So it's a global phenomenon that game playing is up while consumption of traditional media is down. Anybody who is old enough to remember *Pong* as a kid is now approaching fifty, and has likely played a game recently.

Time with a video game necessitates time away from another activity, and people mostly seem to use video games as a replacement for consuming older, one-way entertainment media. So, of course, since many consumers are shifting their time to spend more of it with video games, marketers want to put advertising there, too.

There has been a proliferation of approaches in this regard during the past few years. We tend to view games as another channel that should be used to deliver commercial content, so a lot of old ideas have been wrapped up and put in or around games. It's all very interesting, and some of it is downright amazing. But it's mostly delivering an electrified buggy whip.

I'm not so sure any of the current uses of gaming for branding truly recognizes the potential within the gaming paradigm, nor delivers any meaningful, lasting benefits to the businesses that are experimenting with it. Branding can and should influence, and be influenced by, video games. But, as in the case of search and social media, it'll take more than marketers to figure it out. There's a lot to learn and do here. Let's play on.

MARKETERS TRY TO GET GAME

Marketing has played with the idea of gaming for a long time. Active games, like sweepstakes, contests, and lotteries, have often played an important role in driving sales. Further, many of the activities associated with marketing resemble the qualities of gaming behavior:

• Clipping coupons is a game, if you think about it.

• Searching for a sale item buried in a store bin is a game, as is waiting for the items to go on sale in the first place.

- Collecting and using frequent flyer miles or buyer points is a sort of game.
- Value-add offers in the sale process, like upsell products or shipping discounts, can feel like a game.

Whatever the gaming element, however, it's never *branded* as such. These activities are too dumb, too visceral, too risky, or just too costly for businesses to ever try to make them core components of their branding. In many companies, such activities are not even reflected in marketing budgets, but instead are included as sales or promotion expenses. Games might get consumers to do things, but they don't build brands. They're tactics, and base ones at that.

It's no surprise that marketers look at the world of video games with the jaundiced eye of a disapproving parent. Everyone knows that video gaming is a waste of time. *How* and *why* the game medium works is no more interesting or useful to branding than the mechanics behind contestant selection, or printing and binding brochures. What matters is that people consume games, and as such, they are an audience that should be exploited for the purposes of branding. Content is king, remember, and games are just another *channel* for the traditional model of brand. So we see video games being used by companies for four broad purposes:

1. **Get consumer attention.** You're online, and when you scroll over a banner ad, you notice that a crosshair replaces your mouse pointer. The ad says "shoot and win a free iPod" or something like that. Another ad promises a reward if you identify a picture of the latest starlet du jour. There's no twisted logic involved on the branding front, no internal belief that the game that has you shooting carnival ducks with your cursor has any association with the meaning of a brand.

2. **Give up your e-mail.** The offer is usually a sweepstakes or an

immediate value offer, asking for e-mails in order to qualify for drawings of free merchandise. Interestingly, providing any reward isn't always required. We created a one-page website for a client in Australia and, on a whim, put a box on the page that promised information, some time, about the relaunch of an old, well-known product. We had over three thousand people give us their e-mails. It shocked us just how basic the behavioral prompt-and-response paradigm is to human nature.

3. **Waste your time.** A good number of branding campaigns include some sort of game that supposes to benefit the brand simply by associating it with *fun*. Food products marketed at kids are one of the most active users of this strategy. I can remember the plastic records we could cut from boxes of cereal, or the toys available for mailed-in box tops. The same approach has moved to the Internet, where one study found that of 85 percent of food products marketed to children on TV, two-thirds have websites and a majority of them have some sort of online game.[5]

Ritz crackers maintains a virtual arcade of games on its website. The spooky Burger King mascot we talked about in chapter 1 appeared in video games. And it's not a kid phenomenon at all. I can't count how many clients have told us that they need games on their websites. When they are pressed as to why, the answer is usually, "Because other sites have them."

4. **Broadcast stuff.** There's not a major Hollywood movie release these days that doesn't include a video game. The game releases in particular are an opportunity to extend a plotline, or allow consumers to participate in the franchise (and buy more of it). They haven't been overwhelmingly profitable, but titles like *Scarface* have sold into the millions of units.[6] Games from the Harry Potter and Matrix franchises greatly extended the marketplace for that content, even if the games themselves didn't al-

ways win rave reviews from serious gamers. The reverse is also true: creative content from this channel has driven movie and music development, giving us movies like *Super Mario Brothers*, *Blood Rayne*, and the Tomb Raider franchise. Not great art, but there's money to be made.

There's a fifth, latest approach to games, which has involved the largest budgets and thus the attentions of branding experts: advertising in games themselves.

Microsoft purchased in-game ad creator Massive in 2006, and Google followed in 2007 by buying Adscape. Both are effectively *virtual ad agencies* that invent and place ads—well, the representations of billboards, ads, and other marketing—in video games.

In-game advertising closely mirrors the approach to any other media channel in the real world. There are companies that sponsor or advertise on Internet game sites, so GameZone will run ads while informing you of sites to play backgammon or other casual games. Zango will do the same thing. Product advertising appears (and dynamically updates) in online sports games from publisher Take-Two Interactive, or on billboards along the road in console games like *Midnight Club*. Products are actually *placed*—just like they would be used on a set of a TV show or in a movie—in games.

Puma paid to have its products sold, worn, and otherwise written into the gameplay in *True Crime: New York City*, while a player will hear "Hello, Moto" (Motorola's mobile phone greeting) if his character makes a mobile phone call in the game. A variety of cross-promotional activities appear on the game cases, or are noted in game introductions, like the multifaceted marketing between games publisher Electronic Arts (EA Sports) and ESPN2's *Madden Nation* program, which followed a gamer bus and showed all the required young-person-sports-fanatic shenanigans.

Okay, let me see if I get this:

- Video games are incomprehensibly immersive. Human beings might very well have a genetic predisposition to become very attached to them, something that's just shy of addiction or love. We're talking intense involvement here, and the sort of involvement that passes every test of legitimacy.

- People give video games their time, often lots of it, and over long stretches. They keep coming back, in spite of any number of more important influences in their lives.

- They're willing to spend money on video games, from equipment and software to Internet bandwidth and subscriptions.

- Best of all, we know how to build these things.

- *And the best we can do is muck up games with ads?*

So instead of ignoring the billboard as I drive down the highway near my home, I can ignore the billboards for real products in *Need for Speed Underground 2*. Only it's worse, because in the game I'm not just watching the road, but also *watching myself* drive down that highway. I hop over a cartoon of a Jeep that Chrysler probably paid oodles of money to place in my Tony Hawk–branded skateboarder game, and somehow I'm supposed to care that it's a real fake representation, not a *fake* fake car that's just a part of the game?

We're missing the point here; marketers mistakenly see games as a lowest-common-denominator *channel*, instead of realizing that games are not channels at all, but rather *places*, like social media, only much more immersive. Games are models of places where people live, worlds that have rules, roles, expected behaviors, and even dimensions of time. Perhaps most important, video games are places *where people go to do things*, just like they do in online social communities. Games are built upon creative ideas, but they're experienced with behavior.

The latest branding model for gaming takes none of this into account, any more than it cares about behavior or the particulars of place in the real world. The intense reality of the relationship that players have with games like *Halo* makes the imaginary relationships we presume people have with consumer brand names seem absurd.

But there's more.

Understanding game behavior yields a very different understanding of brand. If actions matter and consumers define brand by their behavior and their communities, games could provide a model for understanding how those behaviors connect. The structure of a brand behavior strategy should have linearity, dependences, and outcomes.

Hmm.

Just like a game?

THE FUNNEL AS GAME BOARD

Alternate reality gaming, or ARG, is the strangest and perhaps most compelling and promising category of video gaming. Well, it's not really video gaming, but rather gaming that extends across all media and experiences.

It all started in 2001 with a game called *The Beast*, in support of Steven Spielberg's movie *A.I.*

The game was a combination of puzzle and conspiracy story: you chanced upon a telephone number buried in promotional posters that, when dialed, told you that "Jeanine is the key." Jeanine was a character identified in the production credits, and if you searched online for her name, you came upon a few websites, all set in the imaginary future world of the movie. There were no rules to follow, no guidelines. You had to literally discover more hints and links, and eventually solve a murder mystery. *The game was to figure out the purpose of the game.* Was it real? The future setting certainly gave it all away, but the interaction was anything but fake.

Another game, *Majestic*, debuted later that same year, with the tagline "It plays you." The plot was about a shadowy government conspiracy (this was the era of Fox's *X-Files* television show), and started out with players being abruptly informed that the game had been canceled. Only it didn't stop. Players were pulled into a mystery by phone, fax, and instant messenger. The game didn't let you go. This was a cool and creepy combination, and it was discontinued after 9/11. But the trend had begun.

ARGs have grown and expanded to involve more activities in the real world, in ways that are vaguely reminiscent of the plotline to the 1997 movie *The Game*. In it, Michael Douglas signs up for a game that proceeds to change everything in his life, to the point where he no longer can tell the differences between game and reality: Strangers befriend him, his bank account gets messed up, and perhaps he shoots his brother. He starts to see the world as a multilayered experience, wherein things may or may not be as they seem. Once the truth is revealed to him, he doesn't know for sure that the game is over.

"I'm not so keen on the term *alternate reality* for what we do," explained Michael Smith, CEO of the UK's Mind Candy, which specializes in puzzles and, well, ARGs. Its first *Perplex City* was a global treasure hunt played simultaneously by tens of thousands of people in 2006. "What we do is a way of telling a story, engaging an audience across different types of media. It's not linear, like in cinema. It swirls all around you, using a variety of communications tools. Live actors, classified ads, group events. Experience doesn't exist just on a computer screen."

Brian Clark, CEO of experimental media lab GMD Studios in the United States, has a similar take. "We've never been interested in machines. We're interested in people, and machines have just been the bottleneck. We design experiences to reach people directly. The web is designed to connect people, so it's helping bring back more intimate, more responsive, more implicit social rules and ways to tell stories. ARGs show you can use web as performance, not just documentary experience. Web history becomes a series of events."

"You can't make a computer cry," added Smith. "But you can reduce your friend to tears by defeating him."

These pioneers are talking about a lot more than video games.

Remember the sales funnel from a few chapters ago? When we add the elements of time and space to it—a layer of the Chronology of Purchase Intent, with each step in the funnel a behavioral moment or event that leads to the next—*couldn't we perhaps consider this progression a game*? No, no, people aren't playing one, at least not consciously. I'm talking about the underlying structure of consumer interaction (or customer, employee, or any audience). Marketing talks about delivering content via any number of *touchpoints*, which are glorified moments of one-way media consumption. We've already discussed why this approach is imprecise and incomplete. Relationships with brands are conceived like falling in love with movie stars, and calling membership in a fan club an "engagement touchpoint" is distinctly one-way.

But imagine a branding campaign as the start of a real-time, ongoing game that involves materials and behaviors that cross between the virtual and real worlds. A game could be the model for a truly interactive experience, involving not only presentational materials and cues but the behavioral responses of players/customers. It would be something like *CRM II: The Revenge*, giving consumers (*players*) a structure that they could follow all the way to purchase, and giving companies (*hosts*) a way to understand and measure those moments. It would transform the sales funnel into a game board.

GETTING YOUR BRAND INTO THE GAME

This is new territory: no planning tools exist in the branding world to create a Chronology of Purchase Intent, let alone to envision moments in the sales funnel as steps in a game. We normally hope for some implicit result from branding, or companies wouldn't do it. It's just that such outcomes are most often left to fate, or other external influences over which the brand gurus claim no responsibility.

Games are exactly the opposite, especially ARGs. Games exist because of real behaviors, which is one of the reasons the alternate-world plots don't necessarily feel so alternate. Using game design as a tool for envisioning and delivering branding would bring the reality of that interaction and control to your business. Interestingly, companies are doing bits and pieces of this all the time. The challenge is to invent a planning methodology that links those bits into a coherent strategy.

The starting point is to envision what a game-driven branding plan might look like. There are five key elements for such plans— let's call them *branding gameplans*—and each would yield hints of how businesses could apply them, independently or together.

Element 1: *Gameplans have goals—a payoff.* They have some desired outcome that is as discernible to consumers as it is important to the designers. A purpose. An action. It's the most important element because there's no game without it. Try playing a video game with no goal, whether a complicated role-playing game (RPG) or something simple, like *Pac-Man*. Sports without a goal line or basket hoop. Play poker without winning hands, or blackjack in which 21 has no meaning. A game without a purpose is just not a game anymore. There are still characters, colors, scenes, perhaps something going on before you, but nothing engaging your sense of engagement. No call to action. There's no point.

In other words, it's a branding ad.

The first step in a branding gameplan would be to articulate a specific behavioral goal. Here's a starter thought: *getting someone to buy something.* It's the endpoint of the sales funnel, the strange attractor that centers all your communications activities. A branding gameplan specifies that goal, just as a game narrative ultimately ends with something like "finish all the levels and kill the boss character," or "find the twelve clues and solve the final riddle."

How you communicate your brand should be no different: there's no other purpose for communicating it, other than realizing sales. The idea that you can maintain a separate, parallel function for your brand is inane. So is the idea that you need some convoluted equation written in Sanskrit to decipher and assign value to your brand equity. The starting point of branding should be the endpoint of your business strategy. *Selling stuff.* You'd be surprised how this approach changes branding development from the moment marketing starts planning it.

- **Timing.** A specific, measurable goal requires a time period in which it needs to/should be realized. Nobody intends to sell something some time or someday. So no longer will your company look at branding activities, such as making brochures or updating the website, as simply ongoing, but rather linked into a gameplan that focuses on a specific result.

- **Cost.** Finite programs allow you to budget them. Brand is not something you budget against in some infinitely costly way, but rather is linked to specific activities with expected behavioral outcomes. Investment is no longer made in brand, but in branding activities.

- **Measurement.** You see where this is going. If there's a starting and a stopping point, and a budget put against it, you can actually measure the results. This is no different than the conception and structure of marketing campaigns, especially the ones that can be tracked in the ROI methodology described in chapter 3.

Element 2: *Gameplans have context.* Context in games describes the places gamers *visit* and the rules that govern gaming experiences. Games are designed upon these principles, and the rules are apparent to the players. A set of physical laws apply, however crazy, so players know the broad ways in which their characters and the game will interact, as well as how the world around them will operate. The context is really a part of the game itself, and as important as the ultimate payoff may be, there'd be no game without rules that players could learn and then choose to behave in ways as they wish.

That's a far cry from most branding campaigns, which are conceived to deliver messages irrespective of context. Branding is projected *at* people. Commercials are written, recorded or shot, and then run in media without connection to the time people might be experiencing them, and oblivious to the presence of other branding trying to do the exact same thing. So an identical ad might be run at 8 a.m. or 12 midnight, because what matters to the marketers is the content or ideas within it, and the broad lifestyle description of the people supposedly watching it.

Publicity mentions of a company product or service are evaluated in absolute terms of what words or ideas are used, not in relation to how many other similarly successful mentions occur before, during, or immediately after. And since most branding is not asking people to do anything other than, hopefully, remember it, this makes a sort of silly sense. It's why most of the ads in your favorite magazine appear fairly identical, or why many of the commercials you see on TV prompt you to wonder, *Why are they showing this to me right now?* Developing a context to your branding gameplan would involve:

- **Routines**. Think of the time you spend in the morning scanning your favorite newspaper or news site on the web. We're talking seconds, not minutes, right? It should make placing an image ad, or anything without an immediately obvious call to action, a nonstarter. The same goes for producing glossy materials for trade shows. Nobody wants to carry them. Why would a PR firm value the mention of the product alone (or not at least make the web inclusion a priority goal, not a "nice to have")? Why would a radio spot include mention of a website, since most people listen to the radio while they're driving? A branding gameplan would design content to exploit these contextual habits, not ignore them.

- **Competitive set**. Consulting firms run identical ads in major magazines. So do industrial conglomerates that advertise on Sunday morning public affairs television. A branding gameplan would never let you run ads that were mirrors of your competition; no branding guru could tell you why your slogan was somehow different, or that your choice of images was unique to your brand essence or molecular structure, when it was clear to you that your branding was identical to your competition. The media selection would be based on where and when your targets are doing certain things, and would be intended to realize your desire to influence those things. Let your competition battle for mindshare. *The gameplan evokes share of behavior.*

- **Outcomes**. Picking when and where you run your branding communications necessitates that you think differently about *what* it is you're saying and hoping to accomplish. A blanket "we hope they remember" goal of branding just doesn't cut it. Instead, a gameplan approach would challenge you to define what action you want the consumer/player to take at any given moment you wish to capture (and pay for) their attention.

Element 3: *Gameplans have narrative flow.* English is read left to right, Hebrew right to left, and Japanese from the top down. Time flows from past to future. Stories have beginnings, middles, and ends. We play games by a series of steps, each of which requires us to do something. The branding gameplan approach would recognize these *flows* and try to exploit the inherent direction that exists in our lives. The sales funnel has a flow implicit in its shape—a funnel, directing a large amount of inputs into a focused output—and its orientation suggests a natural direction to that flow, from top to bottom, as if there's some inherent tendency for consumers to, er, swirl down it. Of course, there's no such tendency in the world. You have to fight for every customer you get, and consumers have the choice at any given moment to opt out of your funnel and into another one. So the funnel shape isn't really accurate in this regard; or, if we choose to use it, perhaps we need to imagine it in the zero gravity of outer space.

Nothing moves through the funnel unless you prompt it and lead it to the next prompt. If you let go or someone chooses not to move, they're not still sliding down, but rather floating aimlessly or, worse, spinning out altogether. The gameplan narrative would not only describe the steps people take along the funnel toward purchase, but also create the events and content that prompted those events, and identify the dependencies between them:

- **Behavioral prompts.** Each point of contact with consumers would not be a place to deliver identical branding, but rather prompts for potential actions. A gameplan allows people to do things, whether *physical*—as in "Check your phone to see if you have five bars," or "Did your last broker statement include a charge for services rendered?"—or *responsive*, as in "vote," "reply," "comment," "register," "edit," and so on.

- **Facilitated learning.** Branding takes a menu approach to delivery; because its expectations are so broad and vague, it shrugs off responsibility for consumers making decisions and calls it being "user directed." But you know how people generally come to the conclusion to give you their money (or you certainly can learn it). Recognize that players will be at different points in your branding game, so your activities can and should anticipate these steps, and your materials address them.

- **Don't talk to everyone.** Let's face it: not everyone is going to be a customer of your bank, drink your beer, or wear your clothes. So who cares if everyone thinks your ad is funny, or if they remember it? The branding gameplan approach suggests that you should risk being more relevant to the behavioral steps of your targets, at the risk of not making complete sense to those consumers who aren't going to buy from you anyway.

Element 4: *Gameplans use a variety of tools.* If you think about it, the word-of-mouth programs are de facto ARGs because they get people to say and do things that they might not normally do (or just wouldn't do as often or as loudly), and thus influence other people's perceptions of reality. Since a branding game plan has a sales goal, context, and a narrative flow, it opens up the entire company, along with the rest of the outside world, for participation in its delivery. Brand becomes not just something that is repeated or applied in other areas of your company, but rather *something that comes alive through all of its functions.* You're no longer talking *at* consumers, but creating experiences that move them toward purchase and then keep them as return customers.

No longer does marketing communications own all of those steps in your funnel; people never reached purchase decisions purely on a diet of ad slogans and Internet copy. While branding was busy defining itself through all of the media it could control (and charging for creating and placing), people in the real world continued developing and reaching decisions just like they always did: they talk, share, converse, debate, argue, test, sample, change, whatever. The gameplan takes these steps into account in terms of designing the narrative, and then frees you to develop branding tools across the enterprise.

What might this look like? We're talking using every company function that might influence your consumers. "Think about games as a model for running a call center," explained Mind Candy's Smith. "Or how about making visits to a bricks-and-mortar store evidence qualities of a game experience?" Brands have to be confident and allow consumers to unlock new stories, new clues, and new ways to interact.

So why not look at customer service, returns policy, and at all of that technology that's supposed to make you more efficient, but instead tends to piss people off? Then you can look at the slightly removed aspects of your business, such as policies and procedures (for instance, have you ever wondered why no airline can get its collective branding head around fixing communications to stranded passengers when the weather is bad?). And you can look at sourcing, shipping, and any operational activity that might have a relevance to the narrative that will deliver your gameplan goal:

- **Redefine integrated marketing.** This is a big idea. Brand isn't applied across communications channels to consumers; rather, your branding gameplan is making you brand come to life in the various steps/events of your brand narrative. So different tasks can be allocated to different media (online for affirmation, placards on street corners for awareness, whatever). What's integrated isn't the combination of media for the same messages, but rather the steps in the narrative, and then how every aspect of your business helps deliver it, as appropriate.

- **Stop repeating the same thing.** If you're not imposing integration from the outside in, then you'll stop saying the same thing in all of your branding. That thought is anathema to traditional brand theology, but it just makes common sense: nobody would play a game if it just repeated the same experience over and over. The brand comes alive in the branding activities, and people engage with it at various steps during the game narrative.

- **Awareness is a tactic**. In the branding gameplan model, awareness is no longer the goal—you're trying to sell stuff, remember?—but it does become a very viable tactic for one or more of the events along the way. The game paradigm allows you to link thoughts, emotions, and associative feelings with actions, so you can finally attach brand perceptions directly to reality. You'll know if some quality of your brand is or isn't relevant to your consumers, because you'll see commensurate behavior at the designated point in your gameplan/funnel (or not).

Element 5: *Gameplans have winners and losers*. The branding gameplan model can feel like it's getting stretched when it comes to winners and losers. But games are never a straight shot to success. Each step is a little win/lose proposition, and that level of risk and engagement is what fuels a lot of the passion people feel for gaming. Nobody would recommend that you risk alienating your would-be customers before they've decided whether to buy your product or not. Nobody but me, that is.

Each decision in the sales/marketing funnel is a chance for your would-be consumers to take the next step toward purchase, or to opt out of the process. This is a fact. It's why traditional branding hopes to avoid accountability for any of it, hoping that by propagating information generically, it'll skip accountability for the sales results. A lot of advertising and marketing dances around the subject, too. Nobody wants to push the would-be consumer, or to somehow negatively influence her or his purchase decision. Yet this runs in direct conflict with the avowed purpose of marketing, and the ideal influence of traditional branding.

How can you move people *toward* something if you don't risk engaging at such a level that some people might actually move *away*? Your sales funnel strategy should be aggressively letting people who don't belong in it—who aren't likely to give you their money—out of the process, hopefully as early as possible. You might be able to use a branding gameplan to focus and hasten those decisions, making it a contributor to your branding efficiency as well as its efficacy:

- **Touchpoints as mini-rewards.** Are there ways to offer would-be consumers some payback or benefit for taking minor steps toward the major step of ultimate purchase? It could be a mini-reward of some otherwise unavailable creative content, a discount toward that ultimate purchase, or something else (and/or a combination thereof). If I've seen an ad that prompted me to look for something on a company website, my next behavior should be incentivized with some additional benefit. *The process of getting to purchase should be as satisfying as the purchase itself.*

- **Events that encourage clarity.** Seeing that techno gobbledygook in an ad tells me quite quickly that the sponsoring company doesn't really want my business, since they're speaking in an alien language. The events for delivering the branding gameplan should prompt similar moments of clarity for the people with whom you're communicating. Does your sample program have to be attractive to every human being on the planet, or could it be structured to help weed out players who'll never finish the game anyway?

- **Rewards for tenure.** Think of a frequent flyer mileage account as the basic model for any relationship. Now build upon it: my account isn't just accrued savings, it earns me special status that makes reserving tickets and seats easier. Where are similar benefits for, say, car owners or home buyers? Why doesn't my bank do more for me than tell me I can pay fewer fees if I keep my balance up, which is a gesture totally in their interest and not mine? Great players should get great, real rewards that *help them play the game better*, not just pay them for their game time.

YOU'RE ALREADY PLAYING A GAME

How do you know reading this book isn't a deftly constructed ARG?

A restaurant called the Reindeer opened near Christmas in London a few years ago and lasted only twenty-three days. But it wasn't a failure. In fact, it was a stunning success, selling out all eleven thousand seatings before it even opened. A hip chef and beautiful people ran the place. After it closed, all of the fixtures, tableware, and tools were sold off. It was "a pop-up restaurant," marketed via a spot on YouTube, viral e-mail, and word of mouth. One of the founders described the branding as following something tough, so that if you couldn't find it, you probably shouldn't be coming.[7]

The pop-up phenomenon is nothing new to retail, which has seen theme stores appear to sell costumes before Halloween, or provide wrapping paper services before Christmas. Main Street fashion designer stores appear and disappear. Art galleries host shows without notice. Parties organize and only people who know how to find them get to attend. Chances are you found some special deals this past year, and you felt satisfaction for discovering them as much as you were satisfied with whatever it is you bought.

These phenomena are all experienced as games, and the branding as the gaming experience. There is no brand equity, no complicated associations or attributes that require expensive, sensitive devices to discern and describe them. No talk about potential, or the what-if of things that may happen. The pop-up phenomenon puts ARG into practice, actually *making real* the restaurants, stores, art shows, and galleries. These brands are *imaginary* until they pop into existence, during which the behavior of people—discovering, finding, sharing, and visiting them—makes the brands real. Then they disappear.

So think what you want about these brands. It doesn't matter. The branding is experience, and the behaviors look a lot more like playing a game than engaging with any traditional branding campaign.

Extrapolate these phenomena to business in general and you can see the potential. Think about virtual businesses, or the networked agglomerations of independent contractors who coalesce to create a product or offer a service and then fade back into the ether. Project-based services. Capabilities outsourced to any place on the planet. Contractors doing the work that employees used to do. In this immaterial, ever-changing landscape, brand names become nothing more than that . . . *names*, behind which a shifting combination of people, resources, places, and times organize and then disassemble.

Consumers have nothing invested in brands outside of their experience, because nobody else involved in creating or delivering them does either. Brand is a construct, a moment in time, no longer some Platonic constant but a flickering shadow on the cave wall that undulates until the flames wane and die. Branding is experience in time, and the brand becomes a series of interrelated behaviors.

Such brand behaviors can be developed based on how consumers find and share information, and on how companies are organized to deliver it. These are the qualities that are going to define brands in the twenty-first century. And increasingly, these qualities are going to be delivered more like games, whether they're dubbed that way or not.

I look forward to playing the new Nike shoe and drinking the new Heineken game. As the jazz bassist Stanley Clarke sang, "Life is just a game, and there are many ways to play."

Click.

CHAPTER 8

It Takes a Company

D o you have a horror story with a brand name attached to it?

Dissatisfaction and complaints are up worldwide, generally. People are less tolerant and forgiving, and there are better ways for businesses and interested third parties to gauge and record their frustrations:

- The UK's government-funded Consumer Direct issues service took just over 1.5 million telephone calls and e-mails from consumers in 2006, up 79 percent against the previous year.[1]

- Seniors in Japan are in some instances complaining three times as much as they did at the start of the decade.[2]

- Consumer advocacy groups, like France's Union Fédérale des Consommateurs–Que Choisir (UFC), are more active now than ever before.[3]

Here's my horror story: U.S. retailer Best Buy had always been my local electronics dealer, so recently I asked a blue-shirted employee to recommend the appropriate multiplayer adapter for my daughter's PlayStation 2. When I got home, it turned out that it wasn't the right model, so I returned to the store to exchange it. The salesperson insisted that store policy was that I pay a restocking fee, which amounted to a 15 percent penalty for having followed the store's advice. I shrugged and said that my policy was to avoid shopping at stores that didn't respect me. I wrote a letter to the CEO and asked for restitution. Never got a word back, let alone a check. I've not shopped there since, unless I've first exhausted every other option, of which there are many.

Okay, I know that it's a little, not-so-horrible horror story about all of four dollars, but it makes a big, scary point: no matter how brilliant the store's branding might be, *behavior trumps branding almost every time.* I may have thought fondly about the brand previously, having seen many TV commercials, or dreamily flipped through more than one Sunday newspaper advertising supplement. But what was the value of all that branding when it came to the moment I found myself in a conversation in which I was the only one who thought I had a legitimate point?

Generally speaking, consumers aren't any more satisfied today with service than they were a year ago. One study suggests that service problems relating to billing and voice-routing systems are actually getting worse.[4] It's not that businesses aren't as effective or efficient as they once were. Quite the opposite, actually: lots of businesses have declared customer service to be a top priority, and spent time and money on it. Best Buy probably satisfies lots of its shoppers, along with doing a lot of other things right. It's just that in a world of networked relationships and empowered consumers, *there's no such thing as an exception anymore.*

Consumers have more ways to interact with businesses, and possess more numerous and easy-to-access ways to switch that interaction between providers. Too much detail and too many variables make every interaction unique. There's even some research to indicate that consumers' learned behavior accessing information online has simply made them less tolerant of imperfection and/or delay when interacting with the real world.

Customer service exists outside old definitions of brands.

I can pretty much bet you have a story similar to mine. A nightmare hotel visit or airplane flight. A frightening online order hassle. A meal that wasn't fit for a monster. A service that had some hidden scare. Whether you bought something from which you expected a lot, which is classified by marketers as a *high-involvement* brand, or something that really needed to do only one thing okay, which would be *low-involvement*, there is one common factor that applies across all purchases: *what you buy is supposed to work*. Interestingly, the role that traditional branding plays in that experience is negligible.

Did your brand horror story get a happy ending? Hopefully, the company did something for you, or informed you of something it had done (or will do). The cliché is, "Actions speak louder than words," and it's more true today than ever. Was the action the business took something originating in marketing, or located somewhere else in the organization? Again, since the only thing marketing actually controls is the abstraction of brand, it's unlikely that it could do much else. "Refund," "repair," "renew," or any other "re"-prefixed verbs that re-quire behavior start in any number of places across the enterprise, oftentimes not even touched by marketing, and certainly not considered a component of the brand.

Conversely, if you didn't get satisfied on your issue, chances are that the company only told you something, and didn't have (or wasn't willing to initiate) actions to back up its declarations, however inspiring and colorfully branded the comments might have been. I wonder how many people you've since told about it. Maybe you blogged? Your *exception* may have become *a norm*.

We see a similar disconnect when we look at *brand loyalty*, which is the positive window into customer satisfaction.

Corporate expectations of loyalty are centered on vagaries of thought and channels of communication, yet the reality of behavior encompasses anything and everything the business does, as well as anything else anybody else does in reaction to it. The best that marketers and sales folks can do is create disincentives, usually economic, to abandoning the business: so we celebrate a great loyalty program like the UK's Tesco's Clubcard, when it's really nothing more than an excellent and very successful sales incentive program.

Are frequent flyers loyal to their airlines, or held captive by their mileage accounts? *Loyalty*—the reasons why people keep giving your business their business—has very little to do with the limited tools of marketing communication, such as PR, advertising, sales promotion, or events. Ask Tesco shoppers, or Apple Mac fans, or dedicated Shiseido cosmetics users. They aren't loyal because of the quality of marketing communications, yet we choose to understand these relationships using all the old ideas and language about brands.

Life experiences are inherently complex and messy. There's no way currently to control the *when*, *where*, *how*, or *why* current or would-be customers will have interactions that tell them something about your business. Customer service doesn't start after people buy a product, or occur only in places you've designated for it. It's not just about handling problems, and it doesn't reside in a single department within a corporation. Same goes for loyalty, which arises from experience, and is rarely bought.

Brands don't just precede purchase, but are reborn and recast every time a customer or would-be customer behaves in a way that relates in any way to your business. The distinctions we make between brand, loyalty, and customer service are not only artificial, but irrelevant and counterproductive to business success.

Customers judge businesses by what they **do**, not what they **say**.

None of this is news to anybody. Billions have been spent on systems intended to strengthen relationships between companies and consumers. Endless books have been written about it. You can't have a conversation at work without mentioning consumers at some point. It's politically incorrect to do otherwise. Yet the salutary coverage is sometimes suspect: the American Customer Satisfaction Index reported reaching an all-time high at the end of 2006,[5] but the details reveal a different story.

Upon closer inspection, that latest level is just about equal to the ratings reported in 1994—when at least one out of every four customers was unhappy—so businesses have spent more than a decade disappointing lots of customers. Satisfaction in many of the industry categories reported is either flat or down. And nowhere in the data is there any indication of consumer loyalty, or of the relevance of brands. Customer satisfaction is measured against the specific performance of a purchased product or service, so it doesn't track product switches, simmering dissatisfaction, or outright resignation. So a ton of money and endless customer service meetings later, and we're still no better at it than we were back in the late 1900s?

You've likely had an experience within the last year that made you forever swear off a product or service. Maybe a business dared you to keep giving them your money, either actively or, as was my case with Best Buy, by casual disregard. It seems inconceivable that companies are equipped with the latest technical know-how, not to mention at least a hundred years of management experience, and yet they still struggle with keeping customers loyal. As consumer behavior increases in frequency and importance to brand planners, the failures of companies that define brand by the old model will become more prominent.

The branding most businesses talk about are great dramas and comedies, which leaves it to consumers to write their own horror stories.

A CLASH OF TRIVIALIZATIONS

Underlying all great science and math is philosophy.

I'm not sure your average marketer has an appreciation for just how profound science and math can be. We think philosophy is our exclusive domain. Our answers come from inspired painters, angry musicians, and befuddled poets, whose personal expressions of emotion and feeling are themselves universal truths, in need of no substantiation or repeatability by experiment. Such details are, well, meant for the technicians who work those sorts of things out. We cut to the chase, those of us who grew up in the liberal arts world, so it's not surprising that branding and marketing have grown up independently from the waves of massive transformation that have washed over the corporate world for the last hundred years or so. We've seen it as *just so many numbers*.

This has led to a communications disconnect far more profound than the silly blather about labels I talked about in the Introduction; while we marketers have spoken about and evolved an entire worldview based on the insubstantiality of brands, the rest of the organization has developed its own language and perspective. So while it's clear now that brands need to be delivered via behaviors across the enterprise, there's actually very little capacity for companies to articulate this approach, let alone apply it. It takes a company, but there's little philosophy or operational structure to get it done.

We explored in chapter 1 how our brand theology was developed. It might help to consider a brief history of what the rest of business was doing instead:

- Schools started awarding degrees in the science of management around the start of the twentieth century, formalizing what had once been an opportunistic vocation into a job description with its own methods and rules.

- Rapidly increasing industrial productivity and capacity required ever better tools to track and manage inputs and outputs, so at about the same time you start seeing engineers who aren't the guys who rode in the cabooses of trains: the need for enough bullets to kill millions during World War I called for a cadre of technicians to study and develop new and better ways to manage production. Broadly called *statistical control*, its premise was that you could reduce the things you wanted to accomplish in business to a set of numbers, and thus improve processes, performance, quality, customer satisfaction, and profits.

- One of the pioneers, Walter A. Shewhart, inspired a young man named W. Edwards Deming. Deming's management ideas helped the United States produce the weapons that won World War II. He then went to Japan during its reconstruction, because the idea of using statistical methods to do better with less, and do so more regularly and profitably, was very interesting to an economy that had little, and wanted to do more. American business was content with the idea that the purchasing power of its consumer markets would take care of any inefficiencies in its operations.

- Deming's statistical approach drove a rebirth of Japanese industry, producing world-class productivity and quality gains that
  were then reintroduced in the United States and morphed into
  an approach called Total Quality Management (TQM). This, in
  turn, gave rise to the wide adoption of ISO standards (for the
  International Organization for Standardization, which originated in the UK) and the Six Sigma measurement standards created at Motorola, which were made famous in the United States
  by Jack Welch's GE in the 1980s and are now a global phenomenon, boasting acolytes at ING, Allianz, Sony, Schlumberger,
  and thousands of other businesses.[6]

- Concurrent with these process developments were various
  technical tools to deliver better management, starting with
  inventory management and manufacturing requirement planning (MRP) in the 1960s, enterprise resource planning (ERP) in
  the 1990s, and a slew of software applications, like Y2K's customer relationship management (CRM), supply chain management (SCM), and any number of department-specific versions
  (including many software tools that promise to keep an eye on
  marketing expenditures).

There's a lot of philosophy behind all these numbers. In fact,
Deming himself registered a not-so-humble name for his approach:
the Deming System of Profound Knowledge, in which he taught
fourteen basic points through workshops, speeches, and books. In
the spirit of deferential impatience, I summarize them into three
truths: *work together*, *constantly improve*, and *communicate*. The
Six Sigma aspirations are even more macrocosmic, requiring their
adherents to become certified at different levels, as if they are being
indoctrinated into a caste of initiates in a secret club.

Never have references to Utopia or the perfectibility of the
human soul seemed more achievable and been rendered less
inspiringly.

That's because these processes and technologies have involved all of the non-poets in the corporate world, utilizing instead the beliefs and expectations of a diverse group of individuals and departments other than the keepers of brands. Not just the manufacturing and finance people, but also operations, IT, business strategy, sourcing, even human resources have participated in deciding to measure what's important, and therefore *identifying what is important to measure*. Each of these departments has then gone on to reinvent itself based on one management trend or another, sometimes more than once, hoping its processes embody the philosophical intentions of quality improvement, CRM, or whatever ideal drives the project du jour.

Central to every one of these management approaches, however, is a focus on externally perceptible and measurable data points. And it's not just these organized management systems that aspire to higher ideals: there's philosophy to it that is implicit in the minds of every manager with a degree in statistics, accounting, business management, or any other operationally relevant subject. It all makes perfect sense.

Statistical science provides the way to know when you've arrived at perfection.

Of course, no management theory would be complete without recognizing that customers buy the stuff that companies sell. Customers are an important cog in the processes of Six Sigma, represented as a statistical variable called *Voice of Customer*, and which might be on par with, say, cost savings on parts sourcing. Customers are a way of understanding an agent of action within the system and incorporating it into process. So people *use* products and services much like a step on the production line might use raw materials and other resources. You can just see the spreadsheet or computer screen that tracks those numbers. "Is it sufficient to have happy customers? The customer never invented anything. The customer generates nothing. He takes what he gets," Deming reportedly said at one of his seminars.[7]

This philosophy is evidenced by the definition of a *voice*, which inherently suggests that it is one voice out of many. Or perhaps this lone voice is inherently squishy and imprecise when contrasted with the other inputs into the system. If anything, consumers stand out simply because they're situated at the end of a long production chain, a point among many in a process. But there is a lot of work that any corporate manager has to worry about before getting something to that spot.

Improvements to be made.

Savings to be realized.

Teams formed and disbanded.

Other voices to be heard.

Profound knowledge to be realized and then put to the test.

The concept of the Customer in CRM software is somewhat different (the C in the acronym promises that the customer side of a relationship can be *managed* by the company side). Just for reference, CRM operates mostly as a technology tool that promises to organize, and sometimes automate, the subset of inputs and outputs that are customer-facing. Its guiding theology is that by using such tools, customers will be situated at the center of an organization's activities, helping give us *customer-centricity*, which is one of those brilliant buzzwords with which you can't argue, but that cries out for somebody to explain it.

The quality and efficiency of Six Sigma or any other statistical management approaches aren't enough in the world of CRM. Now there should be a tool that organizes all of the back-and-forth between the company and its customers, creating an incessant feedback loop. The measures of customer satisfaction in CRM are fluid, but again, they're based on a variety of tangible actions that can be measured.

E-mails sent.

Responses received.

Total cost of acquisition.

Purchases by user.

Once companies put all of that back-and-forth on the same computer screen, they usually see a lot of redundancy and can fire a few people. This is the main reason that CRM software installations have been effective so far.

Wherefore art thou, brand?

Brands are generally outside of such operational management religions and their vestments. Companies have turned themselves upside down, sometimes repeatedly, in pursuit of doing business better and more profitably, all in service to various philosophies that define what success will look like. Marketers have been basically absent from this transformation, keeping definitions and experience of brand an externality, an intangible component of business practice.

Just as we explored in chapter 2, brand can be seen as the ghostly apparition in the séance room. Management scientists show up with their sensing devices, or want to turn on the lights to see what's going on. But we marketers want to keep the room dark, because only then can the reality of brand be sensed, however indirectly. There's management science, and then there's evolved the parascience of brand. And never the two shall meet.

Much of branding's exile from the mainstream of business management has been voluntary. Most companies exist in the material reality of experience and behavior, wherein the laws of physics, chemistry, and causality apply. Marketing, especially those activities that relate to brand, operates on an entirely different, higher plane of existence. Branding is a separate theology, with its own presumptions and beliefs, some of them reasonable and some incomprehensibly fantastic.

Consider your own business for a moment. If you're in marketing, you already know what I'm talking about. Brand is something more, something beyond the technicalities of business operations, right? If you're not in marketing, don't you sense that marketers consider themselves somewhat of a *different breed* than pretty much everyone else in your organization? Are their actions held to different standards, if at all? Are budgets scrutinized and understood with the same granularity as others?

While companies have struggled to figure out how to improve the performance of the gizmos they manufacture, or steal minuscule amounts of cost savings from the production line, branding spends money in service of an esoteric ideal. An *experiment* in the branding world has different criteria and performance benchmarks than, say, a test of a new assembly line sensing device, or the financial return from a new pricing model. This is because the emotional, potential-rich universe of consumer thought is utterly removed from the rational, statistical-based world of business operations.

Processes are trivial to the concept of brand, just as brand is trivial to most statistical processes.

This carte blanche from many of the upheavals we've seen around us has left us conflicted. Marketers have a love/hate relationship with branding.

On one hand, we believe it's something profoundly important, and many minds greater than my own have spent time and effort to substantiate why. On the other hand, the best we get for our belief is often begrudging tolerance from the organizations for whom we work or serve. Sure, branding gets highlighted in press releases and corporate reports when it's convenient, but the rest of the time we fight a rearguard action:

- Our budgets are constantly under attack.
- We are required to make arbitrary, cross-column cuts whenever there's a downturn in sales.
- We're held accountable for immediate sales results and other outcomes that aren't even a part of what we set out to do.
- We feel constantly misunderstood and underappreciated, and bemoan the fact that we're not *sitting at the table* in the C-suite, crafting business strategy with the lesser types from the operational departments.

In fact, we fundamentally don't acknowledge the dichotomy between the pursuit of quality (statistical processes and software tools) and the pursuit of brand (customer perceptions and intent). We don't even have a competing theology to counter it. Many of the management approaches have consistent, agreed-upon criteria by which to practice and measure their work. Branding has no such underpinning to which everyone agrees. We're kind of like a loose affiliation of UFO enthusiasts. The self-help cult EST had more organization than the branding community. And for the past fifty years, all we've done is find new experts, instead of developing objectively real, agreed-upon principles.

Yet we still believe that branding gets at truths that quality processes could never understand, let alone measure. You can just imagine the Socratic dialogue within companies all over the world:

Brand Marketer: Brand is an intangible.

Process Stat Guy: If it's intangible, how do you know it even exists?

BM: Oh, it's obvious. Why do people choose Coke instead of Pepsi, or drive a BMW? Why is Apple so cool?

PSG: What do those products have to do with the industrial widgets we sell?

BM: They're examples of how to do branding. People love those brands because of how they perceive them.

PSG: Perceptions? Doesn't all of this boil down to good products and customer service?

BM: Hah. Not at all. I'm talking about our brand equity. The real reasons people buy from us.

PSG: It just doesn't add up. I still don't understand how brand equity is anything more than the result of how our company serves our customers.

BM: That's why you're not in charge of managing the brand.

Both worldviews are right, but each only partially. Both approaches are incomplete, inadequate models for dealing with consumer behavior. Just as customers are not engaged in the contemplation of brand attributes or in having relationships with them, they're also not residing at the end of a production line or at some imagined "center" of an organization.

There is no center to the organization.

Any and all operational functions of the business are as important to the brand as anything marketing might do. Company activities and customer perceptions are intertwined in many ways—communities, dependencies, partnerships, outsourcing, transactions, product or service experiences—and it is in these relationships that brand and business are realized.

Brand is the verb of these behaviors made relevant to your bottom line.

NOT "OURS"

As if you needed to be reminded, we live in a networked, real-time world. Nothing follows a script anymore, or at least not a static one. There are an infinite number of issues both customers and would-be customers might experience. This means that the outbound component of branding no longer resides in marketing, sales, or any department within the organization, and the inbound component of customer service isn't the exclusive domain of a phone or e-mail-answering corporate function either.

Remember, they're not **your** customers, at least not by any traditional sense of the term.

Today's consumers belong to nobody but themselves, and the behavior to which your business is privy may have absolutely no connection to their other behaviors, other personas, at other places and times. You get a slice of the consumer, at the moment he or she behaves in a certain way that is relevant to your business goals.

It takes a company to establish, interact with, and support the networks of people who constitute a market, an employee base, a supplier and vendor community, and any third-party grouping of friends, critics, or interested others. It takes a company to *be* the brand, not just talk about it or sport the same uniforms.

Doing this is a lot easier said than done. An independent Forrester Report entitled "Reinventing the Marketing Organization," written by Peter Kim and published in mid-2006, took a look at some of the issues and recommended that marketing redefine its role to that of owning not just the 4 Ps (Product, Price, Place, and Promotion), but also the culture and technologies that support it across the enterprise.[8] This doesn't seem like it's going to happen anytime soon, though. "There's been a drive toward accountability in companies for decades already," Pete explained to me in a subsequent interview. "Marketing is the last department within the organization to get optimized, so it's a bit of an uphill battle. The question is whether you change the entire organization to accommodate a new marketing model, or just realign marketing with other parts of the organization."

I think *marketing and the other departments in companies need an intervention*. Branding on one side, statistical controls on the other; like sparring spouses, or negotiators from opposing sides of a war, the two approaches to corporate purpose and performance will never find a resolution unless (1) both sides agree to what the word "resolution" means, and (2) they both want to realize it. I think the rationale for the second point is clear to anyone who is in business today. You don't need this book to convince you. But you do need to realize that the best thing you could do for your branding right now is to stop spending money on that next big branding proposal, and instead take the time (and risk) to look at the totality of your business.

Take a step toward rapprochement, and begin to explore the ways your brand and business are one and the same.

Here are some ideas to help the two sides meet half way:

- **Ban the "B word."** "Brand" is the eight-hundred-pound gorilla that crushes every conversation about itself. Nobody in the organization defines it the same way marketers do, and I guarantee that there's no consensus within your own marketing department about what it means, either. As long as conversations focus on an *it* of brand instead of the *what* of behaviors, you're doomed. Right now, everybody expects the marketers to do what we always do, which is to lecture on abstractions of intention and whatever else we think substantiates our beliefs. This is a broken record. So ban the B word from your lexicon.

Don't use it. Talk about *behaviors*. Marketers can practice by having an internal departmental meeting on a particular program or campaign without using the B word. Try looking at the results from a PR campaign or a trade show without crediting some benefit to the B word, and you'll quickly find that those campaigns usually have absolutely no purpose other than to keep you employed.

Don't have a heart attack, but here's a secret: *the rest of the organization already knows this*, so you might as well stop telling them that they're wrong.

- **Ditch references to "the customer," too.** The process folks have to start off with a significant concession. Chances are that your company has wasted—er—invested money in a CRM software product or some other technical gizmo that promises to manage relationships with "the customer." Your process has a gloriously detailed spreadsheet or slide presentation that defines "the customer" at the subatomic level. Guess what? "The customer" is a stupid, make-believe idea just like the B word.

Marketers know a lot about segmenting, categorizing, and otherwise qualifying customers by various criteria. They know that customers don't belong to your processes—they're not *yours*—and they don't even sit comfortably or consistently in the categories that they're supposed to sit in. Marketers think you are ignorant in this regard (because you sort of are), and your technological prowess doesn't matter to them (in part because they're still struggling with using e-mail). Most of your spreadsheets are nonsense, and you should make your implementation consultants reimburse you (and the planet) for all the resources they've wasted to produce them.

You need to leave behind the idea that you can build a machine to manage things. You can't. The behavioral plans you will hatch with your brethren in marketing will attempt to understand the behaviors of people and groups of people as prompted by a variety of things internal and external to your company. Hopefully you can adapt your expensive systems to manage the processes that enable those behaviors. But presupposing you can manage customers is like playing *Pong*. Don't be a geek. And don't hit a hot button for the marketers.

- **Everybody agrees that there are some things you just can't measure.** People aren't machines, and they're not spiritual entities trapped in corporeal form. They're just people and the desire to monetize and measure what they do is ultimately flawed. We all know that some of the most important things in life defy complete quantification: but *love*, *happiness*, even *satisfaction* certainly have components we can identify, and even behaviors we can prompt and track. That's why you have processes and branding plans.

  But there's always going to be an element to things that you just can't nail or which somehow fall between. You see it when your fellow employees are particularly happy, or feel rewarded by a project's success. Consumers show it, not just by their purchase behavior. Your own behavior will be one of the core attributes in processes and networks you build to prompt and measure consumer behavior. Acknowledge that happiness is a legitimate and necessary outcome for everyone involved and touched by your planning. There will be benefits to your plans that might well be quantified with a deeper color hue instead of a yen or dollar sign, but allow for this incompleteness, too. Deal with it.

- **Agree that you should measure everything else.** Okay, take all of the specific campaigns that already have a behavioral goal attached to them, whether sales, registrations, or inquiries. This is your tactical bucket. Now look at all of the branding stuff— the campaigns and materials that are measured by awareness, retention, or eyeballs, or perhaps not measured at all—and move it into the tactical bucket, with real behaviors attached. If you can't attach a behavior to it, it's not really an activity, but a statement, or hope. So drop it. You want to eventually end up with this single bucket, renamed *brand behaviors*. The rationale for doing this is simple. Making it happen is the rocket science.

- **Change your planning tools.** Like I said, you should get your implementation consultants to go plant some trees as penance for all the presentation slides they've made you endure. But my experience with companies across the globe is that the tools we use to plan and present are themselves damaging to the planning process (or certainly biased toward the ethereal and fantastic).

  There are implicit definitions in the tools: boxes stand for events, states of mind, or something else, depending on the context; lines connecting boxes suggest action, force, influence, or other accomplishment of work, without specifying how or when that action will occur. Boxes and lines on charts tend to simplify when complexity is required, and connect when no connections are present or real. One noted expert says that the effect is to weaken verbal and spatial reasoning, while also corrupting statistical analysis.[9]

  So the branding people can't bring the slides and video clips that the agencies provide to them so they can sell their mumbo jumbo. And the process people can't use the dense slides that their consultants and technologists use to propagandize their work. Starting with a conversation is a far more effective meeting format. Try meeting without a slide presentation as often as possible.

- **Get down to brass tacks.** The actual reconciliation conversation between processes and brand will consist of four broad activities:

1. **Developing a Chronology of Purchase Intent.** This is customer service on steroids. The sales funnel set to music. As we've talked before in this book, it's the linear path your customer—or paths of your various segments of customers—follow to purchase, and then repurchase, your products or services. It's the expression of their relationship with the tangible deliverable of your sale to them, but it includes all of the steps they must take in order to reach that moment. Your collaborative team needs to start out understanding this flow, independent of the branding blather and process inanity you've each already thrown at the concept. What *really* happens?

2. **Create an overlap of a map of influences.** Once you have a working model of what happens, you need to consider *why*. But we're not talking mental states or emotions here; rather, you want to know what are the influences in terms of *where*, *when*, *how*, *who*, *frequency*, and so on. Open your minds to the possibilities that influences happen far beyond the purview of traditional marketing communications. Take the behavioral model of the consumer and extend it to intersecting behaviors, whether originating from your company or occurring somewhere in the world (or in the cyberworld). Find linkages and connections where you may not have even looked before.

3. **Translate the intersections into events.** By "event," I mean an activity that occurs, not a state of mind or a desired outcome (like selling more). It's something that your business can have at least something to do with prompting, whether directly or by a series of actions that will lead to it. These brand behaviors are the moments at which your customers will, ideally, move along the Chronology of Purchase

Intent and, in doing so, evidence the quality and strength of your brand.

4. **Measure it.** Events have qualities that can be reduced to numbers or ratios, which then gives you an analysis tool to ascertain the performance of your branding at any given moment.

Okay, right now you're thinking that the last branding book you just read asked far less of you. Jeez, all you should have to do is think in *new, cool, technoseductive* ways, or hire another branding guru to host sessions wherein your team can assemble polygons of brands or dip candles of branding or something else utterly inane (and expensive). It would be easier to just keep doing battle with the finance people or to decide at the next process management meeting to effectively write off some arbitrary percentage of revenue or profit that the marketers will waste as "investment in the brand."

Nobody understands branding anyway, so why rock the boat?

All valid points, only there's a single problem: the status quo of branding is producing fewer results than ever before, and it's only going to get worse.

The separation between the processes and brand acolytes in most businesses makes a lot of people pretty miserable. It also uses up resources that could be used for selling things for a profit. Without true rapprochement, you are going to keep repeating the mistakes of the past, while an enlightened competitor deals with the thorny challenge of a new approach to brand.

So you won't be able to avoid the impact of consumer behavior, even if you choose to ignore it and go with that neato, glossy branding campaign that just debuted to hushed gasps in your boardroom. Behaviors matter.

Consider this horror story: Early one Friday morning in November 2006, a twenty-two-year-old employee at Kaiser Permanente, a health services giant in the United States, shot an e-mail to every other employee he could find (120,000 computers, by one count), telling them that a $4 billion technology project was grossly wasteful and flawed. Of course, he was promptly fired, and the company jumped into damage control mode, trying to erase the message from the e-mail servers and sending out a carefully scripted e-mail rebuttal under the CEO's name.

But the wheels had already started spinning.

The company's CIO resigned that same Monday morning, although Kaiser officials said it was pure coincidence. Then the fired employee started showing up in the blogosphere, freely giving interviews to whoever would listen. Stock analysts picked up the story, and at least one suggested the story could impact all IT vendors. Then *ComputerWorld* ran a story repeating some of the same things the employee had alleged in his e-mail, only citing instead a 722-page internal report compiled at Kaiser on problems with the technology project. This prompted an inquiry from a California watchdog agency. Kaiser tried to squelch the ongoing story by buying sponsored links for any search results on the whistleblower former employee. It formed a "PR war room." Yet the entire sordid tale reached the front page of the *Wall Street Journal* in late April 2007.[10]

One employee. One e-mail. It didn't matter if the guy was a nutcase or a true whistleblower. His behavioral map intersected with a number of others. The company could not declare itself out of the crisis. I suspect that Kaiser still doesn't know the extent to which the guy's action influenced events along its various member Purchase Chronologies. It answered the delicate and complicated problem too late, and too brutally.

So was the company's branding decided by the marketers and

their beautiful brochures and PR statements? Or was it decided by the processes of IT selection and internal systems management?

Neither.

It was decided and delivered by the whistleblower.

It's a perfect case history of how the process/IT folks can go about their business with little to no involvement with (or interest from) the brand folks beyond, in this story, the occasional PR release on how the system would cure cancer, support world peace, and do whatever else the Kaiser brand supposedly stands for.

Where did an event like this fall within the organization's planning? Somewhere between processes and brand, probably. Did anyone see this employee as a brand ambassador, or influencer of future pricing from IT vendors? He wasn't even on the radar.

It would have been a far different story if Kaiser had looked at its technology activities, and the involvement of its employees and outsourced team members, as one network in a web of brand behaviors that ultimately connected to its consumers. It could very well have anticipated such an event, perhaps even precluded it from happening.

Brand is behavior, whether companies recognize it or not. Your opportunity is to acknowledge this truth, and to begin a process of truly integrating it into your business plan. It takes a company.

Doing so will help you avoid being the company that writes the *next* branding horror story.

CHAPTER 9

The Buzz in Buzz Marketing

If necessity is the mother of invention, then luck—with just a touch of insanity—is the guardian angel of successful branding.

Buckminster Fuller was an inventor, all-around iconoclast, and a Deming-era fellow believer in the power of the human intellect to solve the mysteries of Universe (he felt there should be no "the" before the word, as Universe encompassed everything). His blinding insight came to him well into his thirties, and it moved him to not only forsake a regular nine-to-five job but actually stop talking for a few years and instead invent things to improve the quality of life for the rest of us chattering types.

Fuller couldn't market his way out of a paper bag and had no interest in doing otherwise. One of his first inventions was the 4D House, which looked like a spaceship and had the potential of putting every home construction and design firm out of business. His would-be competitors were lucky, however: his writing style made haiku seem clear, and the rare times he got publicity coverage were when his wife showed his drawings.

Then, in 1929, he built a model of his house and decided it was time to talk about it. There's no report on his subsequent speech at the Chicago Home Owners Exhibition. He generally spoke like he wrote, so the impact was probably slight.

Enter Waldo Warren, a PR guy working for Marshall Field's department store (now merged into Macy's), who thought the 4D House model would be a great prop for a promotional display of new furniture the store had imported from Paris. The flack even asked Fuller to speak several times each day, perhaps thinking the guy's dense babble sounded futuristic. His team of marketers helped rename the house Dymaxion, thinking it would be catchier with shoppers. Fuller subsequently adopted the term as the brand name for much of his life's work

And that life was never the same.

The awareness he gained, both via the media and word of mouth, enabled Fuller to launch an ongoing road trip of speaking engagements that didn't stop until death forced him to cancel the following day's appointments. His newfound confidence moved him to create a series of other inventions—the geodesic dome, for instance, like the one featured at Disney World's Epcot, along with the idea of Spaceship Earth—and to become an advisor to governments on developmental policy. He penned a detailed, all-encompassing philosophy of life (Synergetics, not to be confused with Scientology's Dianetics), which backed up his theories about how Universe was structured. And it turned out he was right about it all; scientists discovered a new type of carbon matter that confirmed his vision, naming it a *fullerene* (also called a *buckyball*). By the time of his death, the Buckminster Fuller Institute reports that he'd registered twenty-five U.S. patents, written twenty-eight books, received forty-seven honorary doctorates, traveled around the globe fifty-seven times, and been nominated for the Nobel Peace Prize.

But how, I want to know, did Field's do with its furniture sales?

It must have been a successful promotion, or Waldo Warren

would have pulled the plug on Bucky. But perhaps the tie-in didn't run as long as planned. Maybe a special order of striped shirts nudged the futuristic house display from the State Street store window. The promo could have run longer than planned—perhaps extended a day or more, because Warren was good-hearted and wanted to give Bucky a chance to make sense, or his superiors were unhappy with the sales results and his job was on the line—which gave time for the right people to happen upon the display and make big-ticket purchases. Had Field's run the campaign the next month or the next year, the outcome could have been very different, for better or worse.

Two things are for sure: first, it was a discrete moment, inexorably linked to the context of place, time, and circumstance. And it just worked out to allow Field's to promote some chairs and Buckminster Fuller to change the world.

Chance is the mechanism for influencing intangibles.

Let's presume, for a minute, that you wanted to model this story and implement the business case of *Buckminster Fuller, the brand*. You've invented something and then go about doing everything Bucky did, down to the minute details. For you to succeed, a PR dude would have to find you. World events would have to cooperate. Lots of other random, uncontrollable variables would need to go your way. Miss any one, and your results could end up completely different.

Brand success is wedded more to circumstance than to the inherent qualities of product or service.

The unknown variables of chance are the ultimate deciders of brand success or failure, and they remain maddeningly beyond the line of sight of the best branding plans. Not only can you not take past marketing activities out of time and place and hope they will work again, but the fact that something worked in a particular time makes it less likely that it'll work another time. Marketers need to be smart, but the real payoff comes to those whose activities are fortunate enough to jibe with the zeitgeist of the day. For these reasons, luck emerges as the guardian angel of branding.

That's why there's no single marketing and branding methodology that works. What succeeds one time fails the next. A failed strategy is mildly adjusted and is wildly successful the second time. Something fails in one time period, but produces mixed results six months later. Brand is rarely a predictor of future success. Movies, music, and books are great examples of this truth. The variable in every case is usually the *why* people did or didn't do what we expected them to do. In the traditional branding world, *behavior is somehow an externality* that can only be understood, blamed, or otherwise contemplated after a campaign is over. Sure, it's a hint, and its proponents certainly make a lot of promises about what it will accomplish (to which they never seem to be held). But brand is inherently backward-looking. Success is often the result of behavioral cues that were left to chance.

Buckminster Fuller incorporated behavior into the substance of his brand. His personal philosophy was that the *what* he stood for was far less important than *what he did*, and what other people did as a result of interactions with him. He had no departments with which to wrangle, and no turf wars about who owned which ways to talk to consumers. He didn't have to legitimize his branding to anyone, or do anything for it that wasn't organic to the substance of his work.

One of his most commonly used tactics was to host workshops (either himself, or by enabling a cadre of supporters, some of whom continue the practice to this day) in which people *behaved with him* and then were empowered to do things differently thereafter. He was actively and intimately connected to the circumstances of his day, and this helped even his most outlandish ideas appear at least somewhat relevant. His branding was real-time.

What if the marketers at Field's had done the same? Maybe history would have recorded Mr. Warren and his furniture sales.

START-UPS MAKE BRAND-ADE

The founding myth of Britain's Innocent fruit juice is repeated in just about every telling of the company's history. Three college buddies wanted out of the corporate rat race and dreamt of a fresh, pure juice company that made it easy and fun for people to do something healthy. So they mixed up a batch of their first recipe, set up a stand at a music festival in London, and literally *asked consumers for their permission to start a company*. A resounding *yes* led them to walk into work the following Monday morning and resign, and gave birth to a business that, as of the beginning of 2008, commanded the largest single share of the UK smoothie market. Everything the company does seems to flow from that founding moment, however apocryphal the story might be.

The thing is, Innocent is not a case history in branding, at least not as traditionally envisioned. Nobody consumes its *brand*. The purpose and value of the business is not its cute logo, talky label copy, hip website or engaging blog, or the funny cow and grass-themed delivery trucks. The company didn't ask for permission to propagate its marketing back in the late 1990s; rather, it asked people if they thought the drink—which was good for them—tasted good enough to buy. Everything about the company is good for its consumers, down to its policies, job descriptions, and physical facility, but it's all centered on a fundamental business proposition: *Drink our smoothies*. Labels, shelf positioning, available retailers, and every other aspect of its business supports this proposition. The brand is only as strong as the number of active purchasers. All of the cute marketing reinforces that behavior.

At least it better do it. The "Smoothie Wars" are well under way across its home market.[1] The Feel Good Drinks Co. produces bottles, imaging, and just about everything else that can evoke a less-than-subtle desire to steal Innocent's customers. Australia's Boost Juice invaded in April of 2007, promising the same general benefits. Lovejuice and Crussh brands have been serving from stores across England, while Dublin-based Zumo has thirty stores of its own (there are at least twenty-four multisite juice bars in the UK). PepsiCo bought a line of drinks called PJ Smoothies in 2005. Other conglomerate moves are likely, if the category that Innocent pioneered continues to grow.

Of course, competition isn't new by a long shot, but the fact that every aspect of the branding is copyable must keep the folks in Innocent's Fruit Towers up late at night. The branding blather about position and meaning is ultimately unownable, at least as a set of tools. Any competitor can blog, post, promote, host, or create cuddly marketing that outcuddles Innocent while it outspends it, too. If they're smart, they'll siphon away Innocent's market share by copying every aspect of its communications, and just do more of it.

Nobody can own an image, but anyone can own a behavior.

The images won't accomplish the same things, of course. Different time, different competitors, and consumers knowing and doing things differently than they did when Innocent first launched itself mean that the exact same branding won't work the exact same way a second time over (or many times over, as each competitor delivers its own version of "healthy," "happy," and "bursting with honesty"). That's why gigantic new consumer product launches fail far more often than they succeed.

So while the branding experts are busy knocking off bits and pieces of its imagery, the opportunity for Innocent is to realize the more substantive truths of *who, what, where, when,* and *why* it prompts consumer behaviors. What can it do uniquely versus its competition? It has a multiyear head start at getting people to do things, so its opportunity is to substantively build upon it with actions, while its competitors wage a war with words and images.

The worst thing that could happen would be that Innocent possessed the best unaided brand awareness, just as it ceded market share to its competitors.

The best thing that the smart folks in Innocent management could do would be to look at its consumer behaviors, and not at marketing, to find its brand:

- **Who.** Do they know their consumers? Not by some broad, demographic-based categorization, like "twentysomethings on the go," or "women, aged 25–60." Hopefully they haven't fallen prey to such standard brand research devices, which tell you next to nothing. We've known this since the early 2000s. In one study, user profiles for leading brands in forty industry categories were compared, and it revealed that there weren't differences between them.[2] You can't categorize the *who* separately from the *what* and *where*.

- **What.** Do they know what their customers like to drink? Not just flavor combinations, but functions, purposes, and roles for the drinks? What would make the Innocent strawberry smoothie better than the twelve knockoffs that will be available on the same shelf display? What other flavors might be a natural addition? One need only remember the Body Shop and all of the incredible invention it prompted with its brilliant products; unfortunately, what was unique to its offering became increasingly difficult to prove, price, and differentiate.

- **Where.** Do they know where their customers do their drinking? "On the go" is a natural for the company's extant packaging, but there might be other places the behaviors also apply. Perhaps after a workout at a gym, or immediately prior to going out on a Friday night. Does a behavior at one moment strengthen the likelihood of behavior at another, so, for instance, is there a three-a-day schedule of drinks that are integrated in terms of total health benefit, thereby driving three consumption events? Marketers call marketing to such events as *occasion-based*, but the behavior approach means using the events as a tool for developing new products, packaging, and pricing.

- **When.** Do they know where else they might distribute their products, and what else is happening at the moments of consumption? It seems that the only relevant co-marketing and/or distribution would arise from an understanding of the *where* behaviors. It will be easy for any large competitor to get on the shelf at a retailer, with labels that are just as endearing as Innocent. So what about home delivery? Office distribution? Machines for health clubs? The competition will also sponsor hip outdoor music festivals (everyone does it).

- **Why.** Do they offer unique benefits that matter enough to people to make them want to buy? This seems like one of those simple questions with a self-evident answer, but the truth of Innocent's competition is that it may not have much to offer except alternate versions of smoothie concoctions. A cute blog will not preserve its market share, but perhaps is a key element to motivating its consumers. Every element of its function has to stay focused on the *why* of its existence: *get people to drink its smoothies.*

The challenges Innocent faces are similar to those of any startup, and by extension, any business, in any category. Whether new competitors are springing up to copy the visible success of your branding, or you're trying to replicate the marketing that you be-lieve led to last year's sales success, the risk of using a traditional branding model means you're likely:

- Looking at the wrong levers of your business;
- Taking them out of their context, and as such;
- Making it more likely to fail, or fail to succeed as well as you'd done before (or as your competitors have done).

Ideas make brands, but behaviors turn brands into brand-ade.

Every start-up knows this, at least the ones that don't have the luxury of patient venture capital funding to create logos or other branding nonsense. Having no money, combined with a fervent desire for success, often necessitates humility, common sense, thrift, self-reliance, and accessibility of the company, its employees, and its relationships with suppliers and consumers. Start-ups need to be fluid and ready to react to unforeseen challenges, much like an airplane flying through pockets of turbulence on its way to a destination. Start-ups acknowledge, by default, that there are externalities beyond their control—for they just don't have the budget, experience, or hubris to think otherwise—and have to plan conduct that incorporates this variability into their functions. Start-ups value real, substantial relationships with consumers (like B2B companies), and grow from that base.

They make do with what they have, and build brand from behaviors; as such, the best drink Innocent has served up is made from the sometimes less tasty, and certainly incongruous, elements of consumer-relevant behaviors, some of which it can control and others which it couldn't, or never will. But it probably knows about those activities.

We tend to forget this truism, this philosophy of the street, choosing instead to believe the more academic approaches to understanding how branding helps businesses succeed. Many of us in business today have never been entrepreneurs, or been in a circumstance to experience a start-up more tangible than a case history at school. Most *how-to* for start-ups is written or perpetuated by *never-dones* who want to expand the necessary actions, instead of compressing or simplifying them.

So we let the media track and celebrate big brands, and talk about brands as if such constructs are the ideas upon which businesses large and small have been built. Businesspeople who should know better let nonbusinesspeople tell them what they are *really* up to, and how to communicate it to their customers.

Ripped from time, place, context, and causal result, we take the lessons of branding and apply them over and over, in hopes that by repetition and fortitude we can overcome circumstantial reality and deliver truths that are forever transferable. Interestingly, I suspect that most successful entrepreneurs ignore the claptrap about brand and identity, or tolerate it as a required, though irrelevant, gesture. Akio Morita, Richard Branson, Steve Jobs, and any other of the entrepreneurs to whom we look as examples of brilliant brand-builders did so by *not following any of the presumptive rules of traditional branding.*

What we should learn from them is not how to mimic their approaches, but how to emulate their uniqueness and their focus on behavior. You can't copy what they've done. We look at what's outside, expressed as *brand*, instead of what's inside a business, which is usually just plain more complicated and rather boring to examine. *Be Bucky*, don't just copy him.

Go check the veracity of my claim. Find somebody who started a company.

You must know someone, perhaps a friend or family member. Ideally, it would be someone who started a business that *did something*, versus an Internet-based get-rich idea. Then ask what mattered: what did they do to build the business? Pay close attention to how the word "brand" is used. My suspicion is that it will be mentioned as the outcome of something the business did, if it's mentioned at all. Ask if things happened that they hadn't anticipated, and how the business responded. What were the core things that determined success or failure? If you did this work yourself, perhaps way back when, or maybe it was your last job, clear your mind and think back to a different time. Think active, action verbs, not states of being. So no *positions* or *statements* or *brand*.

You'll get an earful of something I call *one-room marketing*, which means that companies that are small enough to collect management around a single table rarely make distinctions between *doing* and *saying*. Such business strategy is centered on accomplishing goals and surviving the vicissitudes of an ever-changing marketplace; what emerges *from* those holistic actions is brand, and brand is never set or static. Start-ups and small businesses don't have the time or money to impose it, if such a thing were possible. Some of the greatest, most established brands we know today emerged from this fluid, hands-on phase of business. Kleenex started out as a cold-cream remover, and quite literally tripped on consumers using it as a disposable handkerchief.[3] Video-game maker Nintendo, which competes with Sony and Microsoft, started out making playing cards.[4] Lysol, a brand known today for its stringent, commercial-grade cleaning properties, was once sold as a feminine hygiene product. So much for branding.

Behavior and interaction are central to the experience of one-room marketing, not only in the definition of the priorities it must set in order to survive, but also in a keen understanding of what it cannot accomplish. Yet the accepted mythology of brand and business management celebrates those rare instances when companies changed the way people behave. The power of branding to teach people to behave differently is grossly overstated, and at best an outdated conceit. By far the greater number of business successes come from recognizing and supporting existing behavior.

AIRPLANES AND BEES

JetBlue and British Airways are two companies that were recently forced to deal with the unpredictability and variability of context.

While all companies are vulnerable to externalities that influence corporate behavior and that of their customers, airlines are particularly and visibly vulnerable to the externality of weather. A giant snowstorm in early 2007 hit JetBlue, while fog at Heathrow whacked BA in late 2006. Passengers were stranded, sometimes torturously, sleeping on airport floors, or withering in queues that went for miles. Planes got stuck at the wrong airports, sometimes with passengers imprisoned on them, with no fresh air circulation or hope of departure. Food went bad. Crews were unreachable. Reservation operators didn't know what to tell people.

The crises ended only as they'd started: the weather cleared, which allowed the airlines to catch up, and promise to do better next time. JetBlue made a big deal out of its penance, announcing lots of things it would do organizationally, and put its CEO on the mea culpa media tour circuit usually reserved for movie stars caught with their pants down or fool mouths open.

On April 14, 2007, a couple hundred thousand too many Americans tried to file their tax returns using Intuit Inc.'s TurboTax or other branded software, only Intuit's computers crashed.[5] People didn't know if they'd made the government's most scary deadline. Updates and confirmations weren't available, and there wasn't staff to help people even if there were. The company promised to pay most consumer late fees or penalties, and was still resolving issues a month later.

Good news or bad, these companies had crises because of externalities outside the purview of their brand planning. It's not that they weren't smart enough to anticipate bad weather, or lots of customers filing returns. But the size, impact, and legacy of those variables weren't likely part of a broader conversation about brand. I'm sure there was lots of internal hand-wringing on how the events *impacted* the brand, but they were likely seen as operational issues. The marketing communications people swung into gear to take bullets from reporters only as the crises unfolded. Ads and other tools of traditional branding reflected the news, but remained otherwise focused on all of the positioning blather upon which traditional branding concentrates. The crises, one bad and the other a surfeit of good, made clear not just a corporate divorce from the world, but also the estrangement between departments within the corporations. They became case histories for damage control.

A simple Chronology of Purchase Intent study would tell an airline or tax preparer that inclement weather, or the day before government taxes are due, are make-or-break moments for branding. If you consider behavior as the driver of brand, these influences aren't outside of your planning; they're central to it. A response during either of those crises should have had little to do with issuing a press release, and much more to do with linking behaviors across the enterprise to the outside world, so that the likelihood and impact of such events would be lessened. No supposed lessons about glossy branding communication in a pinch will work in its place. Rendering these experiences as new PR case histories to emulate won't preclude the next crisis. It will help ensure it, which is good news for PR consultancies, I guess.

A new model of brand would involve organizing the company to anticipate and address the variability and unpredictability of circumstance, using behavior as its primary tool.

Forget buying corporate ads or hiring PR flacks to try to convince journalists that bad news is good. Maybe branding is a structural approach to the enterprise as a sustainable, adaptable, one-room branding and marketing machine. Creating something that is almost *consciously alert* and buzzing with behaviors like scurrying ants in a colony, or bees swarming a hive.

Ants and bees?

When it comes to finding and choosing a new nest location, a swarm of bees is anything but divorced from the world. According to researchers, scouts look for sites and then share their findings with one another via complex dance routines. Information is incomplete, sometimes inaccurate, and always changing, yet by working in parallel and with a constant stream of feedback, swarms most often make the right decisions.[6] I think this is why word-of-mouth marketing is also called *buzz marketing*, because it conceptually mimics the process of individuals sharing information laterally, not in a top-down, hierarchical manner.

The relevance of the bees' buzzing, however, is not limited to the communication links it exploits. Rather, it extends to the behaviors the dancing enables, and how those behaviors feed back into other behaviors that improve the swarm's collective intelligence and subsequent movement. Stopping at buzz misses the real impact of the analogy.

Consider that ants are dumb, yet ant colonies are smart. With no central control or sharing of information across the group like the buzz of bees, ants gather food, dispose of waste, and adapt these activities to the exigencies of changing circumstances. They are married to their world, both individually and collectively, and they are so via a complex set of very simple behaviors. One researcher finds that it's not so much that ants tell one another anything, but rather that the pattern of their individual behavior influences what will get prioritized next across the group.[7] So each ant has a function to perform, and the colony adjusts in real time to its world based on the interaction of those behaviors. It self-adjusts, with no central command, no policing of activities, no corporate ID manual.

Traditional concepts of brand are so conscious, so *human*. Most other creatures live very differently; their lives are focused and localized, making individuals of a species oddly empowered to act in certain ways because, quite literally, they don't know any better. Because bees, ants, or any swarming species don't exhibit the qualities of conscious thought, we tend to disregard their behaviors as robotlike. But they are autonomous, flexible, and hardwired to react to their environments, and thereby form a structure that is integrated and responsive. *The colony thinks*, and its brand is *survival*, as with the beehive, or the flock of geese that fly in formation. Every unit in the collective has a role to play.

I know I'm not going to get a lot of points trying to compare brand with running an anthill, but its usefulness as a corollary is shocking. We *think* more, but they *do* more.

Imagine a branding strategy based on this sort of model. It would identify a series of behaviors that constituted a Chronology of Purchase Intent and then, instead of trying to manage the entire span, it would designate the moments that accomplished each moment, assign measures, and then assign a cross-functional team to deliver each of them. Each team would *own* a step the consumer takes toward purchase, as well as the cross-functional business operations that facilitated it. There would need to be some close, interactive system that monitored those metrics for each event, so the team could adapt as circumstances dictated. This system wouldn't manage brand per se, but rather brand behaviors, both by the company and by its target consumers. It would also connect pure *marketing* activities, like placing an ad or issuing a press release, with the supporting *operational* activities, so it would provide a cross-enterprise perspective. It would be fully integrated, agnostic to channel, and light-years ahead of the "dashboard software solutions" that are most often marketed to manage marketing expenditures.

In the case of Intuit, perhaps the metrics on outbound consumer sales would have rung some bells as they went up in the months prior to the tax filing date. This would have prompted the behaviors in support of filing and reporting to get addressed, both from the technical and the communications perspectives. It would also have prompted it to do more immediately thereafter, in preparation for behaviors during the subsequent year. You could just imagine the branding benefits of creating a *pre-due-date filing incentive*, for instance, not only to avoid the coming year's crunch, but to deliver more positive behaviors that differentiated the TurboTax brand. The same would go for the airlines, as the connections between *weather-planes-schedules-staff-supplies-consumers* would be an ongoing map that summed its brand, and thus would reveal needed adjustments in real time. Much of the unexpected would become expected. Fixing little brand-relevant problems would contribute "up" to preserving the brand overall.

It's almost as if the corporate brand could become a living entity, realized by how the company and its customers function in relation to one another, and reaching some ersatz level of consciousness due to the collective value of disparate behaviors within its system. It would allow brand value to become a calculation of the health of this system, at any point in time, versus some absolute, static measure. And it would give companies the capability to marshal all resources to interact with, influence, respond to, and change with the world around it.

Behavior can once again marry brands to the world from which traditional branding has divorced itself.

There are some incredible applications of these ideas already happening around the world. The MIT anthropologist Grant Mc-Cracken has been pioneering a set of vision and planning tools for companies to recognize change and trends, and build movements that feed knowledge for improvements back into the enterprise.[8] His book *Flock and Flow* outlines a detailed approach that works for Hollywood moviemakers and toilet paper manufacturers alike. Sometimes called *complex adaptive systems*, or CAS, the approach is regularly used as a modeling tool in the sciences. One could argue that the emerging social networks we talked about in chapter 6 form CAS of one sort or another. And just for chuckles, you can go further than CAS and start exploring something called *synchronicity*, which can be seen in the ways people, objects, and systems tend to work in coordination with one another: pendulum clocks *learn* to tick-tock in unison, just as electrons will find the same state in which to cohabitate. So there's a behavioral, organizational foundation inherent in Universe that *doesn't even require a living thing to do the behaving!*

This makes our traditional perspectives on brand, however electrified by the latest gizmo, seem like an irrelevant buzz.

STARTING TOMORROW

As we discussed in the last chapter, some companies are already recognizing the behavioral context for brand and are developing organizational and management tools to address it.

Nobody wants to wait, but big ships move slowly, and sometimes, unfortunately, they need to hit rough waters (or a smallish iceberg) in order to focus everyone's attention.

Good luck walking into your next team meeting and suggesting that the department start acting like an ant colony. Yet the challenge right now is to effect change that yields meaningful, sustainable benefits. There are customers to whom you want to sell today, and expenditures you must make that you'd hope are more like investments. Every short-term promotional activity to prompt sales means that you're quite literally *buying business*, or shifting it from one quarter to another. This is a treadmill that only turns faster over time, and your competition can run the same gizmo or trick. The big picture of what your business should become someday is the purview of high-priced management consultants, who have very smart slide presentations on what it all means. You already know better.

You want to be an agent for change, and using a new definition of buzz offers a tactical tool for you to make things happen.

If you look at marketing as an investment in the *behaviors* that lead to repeat purchase, it yields a different perspective than the sort of plan that comes from a *hope* to build some perceptual abstraction of brand. Perhaps you've got it backward. Your tactical actions right now are not just a result of your brand strategy, but the other way around: each behavior is *an expression of the health or illness of your brand*. Who cares if people are thinking or talking about you? The lessons from the start-ups and other one-room businesses are all about building brands based on the behavioral context of your present circumstances. Not declaring, positioning, stating, intending, promulgating, or thinking kind thoughts. *Doing.* The question is how to pull from that theory actionable steps for marketers, independent of any gargantuan change in corporate structure, brand theology, or whatever.

So what can you do to redirect the buzz of activity in your organization starting tomorrow? You can skip trying to change everything, and change something: change how you deliver your current branding strategy.

What you do doesn't have to fit into a multiyear, cross-platform, expensively produced and delivered campaign. Like we discussed in chapter 3, the successful branding we talk about in the marketing world is usually guerrilla. I am a firm believer in taking action and have preached this to clients for years. If your marketing is working on twenty branding-related initiatives, all with various and extended reports supporting them, why not throw down the gauntlet and issue a challenge: Make a difference. Today. This week. Don't mimic the bold language of start-ups, and don't confuse image with reality. *Do something*. Chances are no-body will know what you're talking about.

So here's the question to ask: "What have we done this week that made our existing or would-be customers (or any subset of either group) act differently than they did the week prior?" Moving the brand meter one volt or something doesn't count. But taking such action—*any* action that prompts a subsequent action—has the dual benefit of producing actions that you can measure, while also influencing the dynamic within which your business operates. Don't preserve the brand. Nudge it. Make some buzz.

Behavioral change starts with action, not words.

The tools available to you are many, from the sort of reasonable to the incredibly outlandish and *I-couldn't-advise-it-with-a-straight-face*. I once suggested to a client that he get arrested to prove his point to his customers, and for a moment he almost seemed ready to do it (fortunately, he demurred). I'm not sure that I was totally kidding, either. Start-ups shake things up. They don't differentiate between where program ideas originate and who necessarily owns them. We're talking different seats, next to one another, all oriented around the same one-room table.

What would branding decisions look like if you were to apply this rationale to your business? Here are four thought-starters for things you could do to start a buzz in your organization in, say, thirty seconds after putting this book down on your table:

1. **Nix the next branding activity as delivered by your advertising or Internet agency.** Bite your tongue if you'd planned to call your gurus this week. You've hopefully realized by now that they're not unbiased as to the ways to accomplish the task of

branding. It should be curious to you that every brand strategy from your management consultants ends up being an advertising campaign, online or off. Letting agencies control creative and media is like letting real estate brokers design houses, and then tell you where you should live.

So don't approve the next branding exercise. Be random. Capricious. If you're tasked with helping to create it, just stop and ask *why?* Programs that will have an immediate negative impact on your business if they're not implemented will be defended; you will be surprised on how little of what's planned actually can argue for such relevance. If you don't spending money on it today, that's a day of costly spending that you've avoided. Same goes for skipping a day of implementing a branding campaign. If you can't prove it *makes* you any money, you can at least point to *savings*. Just say *no*.

2. **Force a translation of IT's latest innovation.** Check your e-mail in-box. There's likely a directive or update on the latest productivity or enablement implementation of some software tool, application, or gizmo. Get the brains that had been working on that latest external branding campaign that you just delayed or nixed, and put them on this project. Challenge them to translate the *change management* component of the project into a marketing strategy that delivers active, happy users in a specified period of time. Nix the education; make it build on behaviors. Then sit back and see just how hard it'll be to do. Any accomplishment in this regard will be an improvement in your brand.

3. **Make marketing and finance trade staff.** Like warring feudal states marrying their noble children to one another, these two functions need to be better linked. Designate a junior staffer in each area and swap them, along with a few specific responsibilities: first, each of them should write a daily, uncensored

blog on their experiences; second, each should have to make a weekly report to their original departments on what they've learned, perhaps tracking a specified list of subjects so they can start seeing progress week to week; and third, each should start, as of day one, recommending ways to improve the performance of both their host and original departments.

4. **Don't assume twentysomethings have the answers.** In other words, don't do the next thing because someone younger than you tells you to. Using our personal, subjective experience has always been an easy reality check, although it has never really been a good source of original research or understanding. Most of the great brand successes that exploited the housewives of the 1950s were hatched by primarily white, middle-aged men. So if you're over thirty, you can stop questioning your own gut, and discard that comfortable, faux *I-don't-understand-the-strange-ways-of-this-modern-era*. If you're a twentysomething, drop the presumption that your age, naiveté, taste in music, or any other personal quality supersedes the value of experience, insight, and openness to information that will yield smart business choices. Sorry. I spent my twenties believing things were otherwise, too. Everybody can be smart about this stuff, only then we grow up. Replace the next "'cause you have to" with research on real behaviors.

Okay, you're thinking all of this is impossible. You have nothing to do with marketing, so there's no natural place to start. Or you work in marketing, but these enterprise ideas are too mammoth woolly to initiate. Perhaps you're still not convinced that it's necessary (or worth the risk to your career).

So don't look any farther than marketing. When you put down this book, there are actions you can immediately take to: (1) better direct your money at behaviors, not just ideals, (2) yield smarter choices about how to make those behaviors happen and then to operationalize the results, and (3) build a more open and flexible approach to anticipate and respond to the changes that real-world behaviors effect.

Maybe your first steps toward a new definition of brand should be tactical. Here's a starter menu of things to consider, any of which could get the ball rolling:

- **Research behavior, not feelings.** We've already talked about the utility of customer segmentation, but it needs to look at behaviors and not necessarily demographics of lifestyle or psychic states. Try to add this dimension to an existing segment—it might be very interesting to see how your segments filter into a series of behaviors. Or craft a new segmentation with behaviors as a starting point. A nice place to begin might be *current customers*. Add this dimension to focus groups scheduled for next week.

- **Impose order on the chaos.** The Chronology of Purchase Intent can be your operational model of the process consumers follow to discover, research, affirm, test, purchase, and repurchase your products. Online, it's a simple tracking of clicks, but in the real world it's a messier, more imprecise model. Start building one, with an eye to order and dependencies. Make it little, but make it a part of the campaigns that the team is developing right now; if the agency just submitted a plan, ask them to add it.

- **Buy moments, not channels.** If you haven't already thrown the *eyeballs* or *clicks* models out the window, you should. Presuming you can find people by appropriate lifestyles is an old idea. Instead, look at your media buy as a tool to prompt the right events as identified in your Chronology. Don't pay to tell people things; pay to provide them with prompts to do something, like *request, enter, check, vote, play, join, exchange, add, inquire, plan, test, compare, reply, personalize, share, modify, replenish, respond, anticipate, repeat, buy.*

- **Add a time element to your campaigns.** If you start prompting behaviors, you can track them, and thus build and check models on the productivity of your branding. Instead of presuming that there's a gravitational force dragging your customers down through your sales funnel, you're now providing that movement (with behaviors) and can track it through time. So every press release has an *end date* and desired behavioral result, for instance. Those brochures you're preparing for the trade show next month? What's the deliverable, and how are you going to achieve it?

- **Nix an associative idea in your brand creative concepts.** Find the most recent or obvious example of a branding creative idea that requires consumers to associate some thought or emotion with your company name or product. And nix it. We already know that people don't associate unrelated ideas like we'd hoped, and if they do, it really doesn't impact their behavior. If you get someone's attention, why waste it with being too abstract? There's something you're doing right now that you don't need to be doing right now.

- **Shave 10 percent from your branding budget.** Yup. Arbitrarily designate 10 percent from the money you haven't committed. Be particularly ruthless with program elements that have no realistic hope of accomplishing anything beyond putting some good karma into Universe. Put the money to the side. Either you'll use it to respond to an opportunity in the marketplace once you have some of your behavioral processes in place (and you may spend it on branding that comes from somewhere in your company other than the marketing department), or it's at least a 10 percent savings on your spend. I bet you won't even feel it.

Can't you already feel it? With a little luck and just a touch of insanity, maybe you can turn even the slightest action tomorrow into a contributor of branding success.

Buzz.

CHAPTER 10

The Emperor's New Clothes

Believing isn't seeing.

There's an inherent tension between what we *expect* and what we *experience.* At times the gap between the two can be great. Our hopes can flavor or sometimes overcome, what we perceive of reality. The language we use to describe these interactions is distinctly sensory-based: preconceived notions can *cloud one's judgment*; ignoring reality means someone is *out of touch*; refusing to acknowledge the truth means being *blind* or *deaf* to it.

But our expectations cannot permanently overcome experience. I can believe that my new vacuum cleaner will make me a better party host, but if my guests don't agree, I'll eventually buy a competing product. If my soap suggests it can make me look younger, or my choice of fabric softener can make my family happier, at some point I will discover whether either promise is true. My imagination that a beverage is the most hip thing ever concocted won't keep me buying a drink that doesn't taste good. The qualities I believe about life ultimately depend on what becomes known to me, whether through my experience or that of others.

If seeing is believing, knowing is doing. Behavior is the statement and measure of truth.

Traditional brands live in that gap between expectation and experience, filling it with attributes and associations that have little connection to reality. It's almost a *brand interlude*, in which the promises of corporate marketers are, for a limited time, believable. "Hope springs eternal" is the cliché that accurately reflects our all-too-human penchant for wanting things to be different than they actually are.

Consumer purchase decisions are imperfect because we often buy in the mistaken belief that our behavior will be different than we know it will be. This is what most branding targets. Direct television advertising—compressing the introduction and buying ends of the Chronology of Purchase Intent into a single event—is the best example of it. But all of branding relies on the interlude, however it's defined by content or time.

That brand interlude is rapidly disappearing. I don't need to experience a month of leaving my Thighmaster abandoned in the closet to know that buying it won't change my behavior; I can read about it in a chat room, or perhaps since then I've already bought two other devices on late-night TV and know better. Years of drinking the beer du jour tell me that single women don't prefer guys who drink one brand name over another, no matter how memorably otherwise the commercials might claim. For any purchase that requires a significant amount of money out of my pocket, I can search online for enough information to be positive of my decision, whether hopeful or not.

Previous generations of consumers effectively lived in a brand interlude that was longer, slower, and more forgiving. Now, once I decide something doesn't live up to its promises, I can inform the world—or be told—about it in a nanosecond. Companies have less time to make good on brand promises, and need to do so more often. The truly believable, sustainable way to make good on brand promises is through behavior, whether that of the consumer in experiencing the product or service, or that of the company in supporting it. Promises of world peace or a better love life are hard to substantiate, so they have little value as currency in the behavioral exchange that evidences today's brand truths. Relying on such abstractions of traditional brand awareness is like watching only the afterimage of this interlude, left to fade, change, or disappear with every blink. Its conclusion, foregone; its utility, negated.

When you look at branding as the ethereal, impermanent intangible it is, spending money on it sure seems like a losing proposition. It's like describing the fine print of a pattern that exists only when you choose to look for it, praising color coordination that appears in certain light but not others, or buying new items in sizes and arrays that have no connection to material experience. "Managing intangibles is hard, and getting harder," according to Jimmy Brown, Ph.D., a management researcher and consultant. "Truly successful organizations are managed with a systems-based approach, including real-time integration with customer experience and the other inputs from the marketplace. This systems-based view enables these organizations to anticipate their customers' needs, which allows them to drive a more favorable customer experience."

Actions speak louder than words. And believing is wishing, not seeing.

A MODEST PROPOSAL

This book is all about creating a new philosophy of brand, which will enable new ways to build and deliver branding. There is a growing universe of people putting aspects of this vision into practice. Behavior is the central tenet as:

- A **management philosophy** for overall business practice.

- A **strategy** for how you understand your consumers.

- A **tactic** that can drive your activities to engage with consumers, employees, or any target.

- An **organizational tool** for structuring teams and identifying objectives.

- A **measurement** for the efficacy of business, marketing, and personnel activities.

Let's recap the line of reasoning that has driven each chapter of this book using real-world examples to form a "modest proposal" for you to consider:

- **Change your definition of brand.** "There are common misconceptions about branding," explained Craig Merrigan, vice president, marketing strategy and design at Lenovo. "People think that branding equals advertising, or naming management. Lenovo understands brand to be what a customer thinks and feels about a company and its products. Therefore, every touchpoint counts, because they all impact this impression. You have to manage what the customer hears (advertising, PR, web), but even more, what the customer experiences (product, service, surprises). And the most powerful thing to remember is that a brand, over time, will converge with *reality*. So you manage the brand by managing reality, building the brand intent into the business and its actions. Say whatever you want in ads, but eventually reality will catch up with you."

  Lenovo is what I'd call a *global, post-brand* business, in that it's not trying to deliver a business model originated in one country or sell static brand attributes based on a particular nationalistic or cultural bias; rather, it's truly a worldwide enterprise, with a local presence in markets ranging from the smallest emerging economies to the largest, most developed countries. Its brand is very much defined and promoted by the behaviors—the actions, via product development, services, and support—that Lenovo can apply within and across such a diverse world of business needs.

Of course, its foundational strengths are important and consistent, like its technical know-how. The ThinkPad product name has been a useful tool too. But no attribute can forever be attached to a product, regardless of the amount of money spent on branding communications. Leveraging its *behaviors* across markets to both define and enable the delivery of its brand is its bold new model.

Consumers demand nothing less, and often a lot more. They buy *things*, not *ideas*, and to confuse their thinking with meaningful behavior is what yields entertaining, memorable branding that produces no sales. Nobody has a relationship with a brand. The *brand interlude* is not an absolute, all-encompassing quality imprinted upon experience, but rather the introduction to it. People are too busy, distracted, critical, and empowered to be easily or continually convinced by the declarations that constituted the Golden Age of Branding.

It has been replaced by an interaction model that is more like the qualities of commerce in the Middle Ages, irrespective of all the new terms for how it's applied: local, customized, constantly in touch, community-affirmed, needs-based, and transactional. Any branding that doesn't reflect this new/old reality is a waste of your company's money.

- **Claiming otherwise is like hunting for ghosts.** Defining brand as an *intangible*, removed from the messy and oftentimes unpredictable vagaries of human behavior, dooms it to irrelevance. A vast industry has evolved, made up of smart, dedicated people who strive to find evidence of brand in thoughts, emotions, and even the biochemistry of the human brain. Yet detached from the behaviors that can be delivered by the activities of your business, finding and measuring brand is no better than attending a séance and hoping to prove it real. Or like a great poet who writes paeans to idealized love, but neglects the affections of her spouse or children. There are no accepted ways to locate or consistently track brand as anything more than associated intangibles, or traces of past events, like trails in a cloud chamber.

According to marketing ROI guru Jim Lenskold, "The problem with brand measurements is not the measurement methodologies, but the fact that many marketers lack clarity on what outcomes they expect, at what time, and how that ultimately influences short-term or long-term contribution to sales. What's even worse is when marketers introduce meaningless metrics such as *advertising likability* or use some such analysis of brainwave impacts. When you measure your success with *feel-good measurements*, you'll optimize your marketing toward those metrics, and not be aligned with business objectives."

If you look at the sales process—call it a funnel, or pathway, or Chronology of Purchase Intent—and translate or attach all of the branding intangibles into specific, targeted behaviors with specific, tangible outcomes, you get a very different model. This would fundamentally change the way you approach your brand planning, shifting focus from the supposed mental states of your consumers to the actual behavioral facts of their experience.

Awareness, whether at the start of the process or at any point throughout, would be no longer a *quality* with an imagined, absolute value, but rather a *quantity* that was a real, adjustable input to the function of your business. You'd never again run an ad that had great recall but accompanied flat sales. Or at least you'd have a measured basis from which to make a better decision the next time.

- **True guerrilla marketers already know this.** "The most successful branding is self-directed," said Brian Clark, resident thinker and leader of experimental media lab GMD Studios. "So when GM wanted to promote its ethanol vehicle development, we delivered a campaign called 'Who Is Benjamin Stove?' Consumers who discovered our character learned about crop circle messages from aliens, and could participate in an evolving narrative that ultimately prompted our client to *respond* to it with information about its alternate fuels program."

According to one news report, the four-month program involved almost 400,000 consumers who spent an average of nearly seventeen minutes per website visit, which is just about the number of people who would passively watch a prime-time niche cable TV show.

Some of the great early guerrilla marketers, like Nike or Virgin, evinced this understanding that behavior matters more than declared intent, and in doing so rewrote the rules for how businesses establish and actualize public awareness. Yet tools like engaging with athletes to co-promote products (as Nike does), or throwing crazy publicity stunts (like Virgin), have become the norm for corporate branding programs. They've become actions that focus on awareness as an absolute measure of brand, divorced from the behavioral outcomes that can be linked back into a business strategy. Today's true guerrilla marketers go beyond that, focusing instead on habits, examples, and involvement to deliver their goals. Behavior is their tool.

And when behavior is an organizing principle, brand becomes something that is delivered over time, and actions become a potent tool for organizations. GMD's Clark explained, "We developed rules for our campaigns, like don't touch a topic the first day we see it, because you don't want to throw gasoline on a fire. There were rules for how we addressed events, so for instance, we would reply to a blog entry first with a simple entry noticing it. The *how* of branding is the prompt for the *what,* in that they're intertwined. Storytelling is 24/7 in this mediascape."

- **Search redefines brand as asking, not telling.** According to Ron Belanger, vice president of agency development at Yahoo!, search is fundamentally rewriting the rules of branding. "Starting with brand awareness, it's important to understand that search is a tool often used by consumers with newly created need states. For example, first-time parents, newlyweds, first-time home buyers, retirees, and even people with a recent medical diagnosis all share the same state of having needs that are new to them. Search plays a major role in every stage of the buying cycle, from awareness and consideration, to comparison and purchase. Some smart marketers are actually going beyond the purchase point by leveraging search marketing as a retention and customer loyalty tool. This is very early on, and we're going to see traction on it."

The search dynamic enables consumers to forever wrest control of brand from companies. No brand is static, nor can it be declared or relied upon to exist without constant interaction and change. Search—as in asking for information and applying it to decisions that then prompt other questions and actions—thus becomes a model not just for web-related activities, but for *any* interaction between company and consumer (or within the company, whether with employees or a supplier network).

Rarely, if ever, is search about finding branding information; rather, the action of search is itself a branding behavior. Corporate websites are rarely the best destination for consumers looking for an answer to a specific question. Search technologies are going to get better at providing *relevance* to queries, which will further compartmentalize brand within each discrete search moment. Building brand will require businesses to link those moments.

"The research suggests an immense opportunity," Belanger continued. "We've found that 79 percent of recent auto insurance purchasers said that search *introduced them to brands they were previously unaware of.* Another survey found that 56 percent of travel searchers said they went to a site they didn't originally intend to because it was at the top of the search results, and 27 percent of that audience said that one of these newly discovered brands had made it to the short list and was being considered. This really shows the power of behavior—matching the right message, at the right time, to the right user."

- **Entertaining consumers is just a distraction.** "Brands will increasingly become content producers," Antonio Bertone, Puma's group functional director of brand and marketing, explained. "Traditional content producers, such as TV networks, used to be barriers between advertiser and consumer. But now we're migrating to a different competitive set. We want to use media to be a facilitator of experiences, not as a sponsor, but as an enabler. That's how we look to add value to our consumers. We don't just talk about being cool, or create things for the sake of entertainment. We're delivering proof points of Puma's difference. So you don't just get to design new shoes on our website, but you also find out that we're making your life simpler by giving you designs for running shoes that fold down for travel and have a space for a hotel room key, or tips on where to spend time on and off the golf course on your next trip to Shanghai. We want to make you smile, but we want to deliver something useful as well."

Promoters of the old branding model are still hopeful that new-media technologies will let them extend the creative-driven, *brand as entertainment* approach, giving stupid network TV ads an afterlife as stupid mash-up videos online. They're encouraged that virtuality lets people take the pieces of branding and transform them into artifacts, or props that can be featured on personal web pages or forwarded to friends. Yet this dynamic reduces those artifacts to meaningless symbols, not the badges of brand awareness or loyalty to which marketers aspire. And sending more entertaining garbage at people without linking it to behaviors that are meaningful—whether to their own interests, from searching for information to having great experiences, or to your business needs, i.e., *selling things*—is just distraction.

"Brand becomes very dynamic," added Bertone. "You need to constantly surprise and engage. At Puma, we try to throw a curveball every time we think consumers are settled on a point, or our branding feels at all static. So when we announced our entry into the 2008–09 Volvo Ocean Race, people probably scratched their heads and wondered what does an athletic shoe company have to do with sailing? But we like that. We want our behavior to prompt interested behavior among consumers. We challenge with new things, while other companies try to reinforce whatever it is they hope consumers already know."

- **Consumers are outsourcing consent.** Marketing exec and blogger Greg Verdino says, "I love the notion of outsourcing consent, but it really isn't the first time people are doing it. Only the nature of *who* and *how* has changed. Before the inception of social media, people typically made decisions by talking to family or friends, consulting with an authority figure, or checking with an expert. If you liked the look of a truck, you might look around to see if any of your buddies drive that truck, then check *Consumer Digest* to see what their experts have to say about it. You still do that, but now we've also entrusted decision-making to this unknown mass of strangers who author online reviews, write blogs, or participate in message boards but, in effect, have no clear authority on the subject.

  "This is a fundamental shift. Instead of asking three or four people you trust, you go to a favorite website or community to see what a number of people you don't know are saying, or check the overall blogosphere on positive or negative comments. There's a difference of scale, as well as time allocation, both in frequency and duration."

This behavior makes a case for the real importance of content creation, whether online or in the real world. Brand consideration might be triggered by search, but social media is changing the way it's affirmed. Most marketing still looks at this phenomenon as either a *channel* through which advertising can be delivered, or some imaginary creative *conversation* about brand. Yet real communities are where brands are tested and endorsed; all of the extended directories, networks, clubs, and other aggregations of individuals—or gatherings of divisible aspects of personalities, so there's no "the consumer" visiting a single site or chat room—serve as nothing more than inputs into this new reality. Engaging the consumer in conversation without an ultimate behavioral purpose that leads to an eventual sale risks being a waste of company money or, if heavily pursued, a potential detriment to brand. Conversely, embracing it has implications not only for external communications but also for internal company structure.

- **You need to do things to influence behavior.** "Companies are starting to think from the beginning about how to integrate the game paradigm into marketing campaigns," said Dave Szulborski, blogger, consultant, and author of the seminal *This Is Not a Game: A Guide to Alternate Reality Gaming*. "We're just now starting to see how games can integrate into everything else a company is doing. For instance, when we promoted the *Transformers* movie (2007), we turned the entire campaign into an immersive experience. It wasn't limited just to an online game, as we buried clues in other advertising.

All of the parts were complementary. Extending this into the organization is a great, undiscovered territory to define and deliver brand."

Once you see your consumers' Chronology of Purchase Intent as a pathway of linked, codependent behaviors, the idea that the brand can be structured much like a game has a lot of power. The qualities of discovery, self-guided authority, personalized pacing, intermediate rewards, and the challenge of skill and luck are themes that keep coming up in descriptions of search technology and new media, and across our cultural landscape. Marketing that uses games as a diversion, or as a trick to capture consumer attention, is a waste both of company money and consumers' time. The marketplace will become less forgiving of this sort of pursuit as consumers get ever more used to possessing the manual for how the new game is played.

The game paradigm has interesting applications to the definition and delivery of brand within the enterprise, too. Games involve more than ideas; there are pieces, places, times, events, and a host of other experiences that, if translated to the corporate domain, extend far beyond the purview of communications tools controlled by marketing. The entire company is involved in delivering such experiences.

- **Get the entire company involved.** Hyatt's Tom O'Toole, chief marketing officer, has long been ahead of the transformation of marketing. "We have a unified perspective of our marketing and use of information technology because the emergence of the Internet, in addition to other developments relating to the business applications of customer databases and information systems, outmoded the conventional functional distinctions of marketing, distribution (reservations), pricing and inventory management and information technology. When, in the mid-1990s, we began linking Internet marketing, such as a banner on Yahoo!, through a booking engine directly to our central reservation system, for promotional offers or rates that were revenue managed, the previous functional boundaries became arbitrary at best. This functional integration has since been furthered by applications of customer database–driven marketing through the Internet, and other developments that are based on the integration of marketing applications with information technology.

"Being responsible for Hyatt's marketing and also for the company's information technology, and thus exposed to both worlds, I noticed a series of interesting phenomena. First, the software vendors calling on us in my IT capacity were often featuring applications that were for, or closely related to, marketing. Business intelligence (BI) applications and, more broadly, customer data analytics were what I first noticed. The sales presentations by IT vendors to the IT staff could just as well have been being presented to the marketing staff. Articles in IT trade magazines about BI applications could have run in marketing trade magazines. Then it really became evident when I spoke at a conference of CMOs and most of the exhibitors in the trade show hall were software vendors for customer analytics and related applications, who were also calling on me in my IT capacity. Plus, it was interesting to observe that at IT conferences and marketing conferences, both functions were struggling for credibility in their companies, often featuring similar panel topics. Finally, both began to feature conference presentations on 'How marketing can work better with IT' or 'How IT can work better with marketing' or other variations on how the two functions can work better together. I was in an interesting position to see the picture from both sides.

"At Hyatt, by the nature of our business and marketing today, the marketing and IT functions are very interrelated. More broadly, marketing, reservations, customer service delivery and information technology are very interrelated and becoming more so. Marketing is directly dependent on IT for customer database applications, Hyatt.com infrastructure, and other developments. Our customer service delivery innovations such as PDA check-in and Econcierge increasingly are IT-enabled. So having the marketing and IT functions organizationally related and, ultimately, the responsibility of the same function head has very practical advantages. It enables us to align priorities, integrate efforts, enable innovations and ultimately be more functionally effective for the business. It can enable breaking down parochial thinking by the respective functions.

"Relating the marketing and IT functions enables data-driven marketing and thus customer-driven marketing. I think that it is essential to the transformation of marketing for the future."

The greatest challenge organizations face is bridging the internal distances between departments, and especially the gap between marketing and the units that are driven by statistical processes. A unified technology platform, infused with the focus and priorities of marketing as evidenced by Hyatt, is one of perhaps a number of ways to facilitate that rapprochement.

- **Marketing can start doing things differently today.** "Our organization is becoming more customer-focused," explained Richard Getler, L'Oreal USA's Interactive and eBusiness Strategy leader. "With more than twenty distinct brands, we engage a variety of consumer segments, from luxury to mass market, from salon professionals to dermatologists. We continually explore new opportunities to expand beyond our traditional marketing channels and messaging to find ways to be closer to our customers. We strive to tie these marketing efforts to measurable outcomes and behavioral goals. We know that to be successful, our brands must ultimately share control with their customers and evolve the brand DNA together."

The idea of constant engagement based on behaviors can be an empowering concept, but marketers often translate the challenge into the old deliverables of brand. The challenge is to challenge the very preconceptions of brand and, as L'Oreal is testing through experimentation, to devise new ways to deliver meaningful, passionate, forceful experiences to consumers. Perhaps the smartest thing marketers can do, irrespective of the efforts anywhere else in the enterprise, is to simply stop doing a percentage of what they believe constitutes branding. The likelihood is that this will not only save money, but afford the planning space for inventing new programs. The best advice is to simply *do something* other than spend new money hoping to breathe life into old ideas about brand.

BRANDS BEWARE

It's almost impossible to believe that companies would choose to spend money in hopes of inventing vague brand-emotional or other esoteric associations. Without specific links to behaviors, awareness is a broad, generic sinkhole for corporate expenditure. Assigning brand benefits without causal proofs is lazy business management, at best. Promising them without delivering real, tangible benefits borders on hypocrisy. This behavioral reality underlying brands today is what makes the anti-brand movement such a joke.

There have always been parodies of branding and commercial culture. In Victorian England, Charles Dickens wrote *A Christmas Carol* as an indictment of consumerism, among many other human foibles. In the United States, *Ballyhoo* magazine published cartoons and mock ads in the early twentieth century: one promoted a toothpaste that was ineffective but cheap, so that purchasers could use the money they saved to buy fake teeth; another promised (with tongue in cheek) placement of phones in such strange household locations as bathrooms. Comedians like Louis Nye and Stan Freberg created funny skits and songs in the 1950s, such as the hilarious *Green Chritma*, which featured an ad agency contemplating ways to exploit the holiday (a reincarnation of Bob Cratchit is the voice of reason in a boardroom run by a money-mad exec named Scrooge). *Mad* magazine's puerile satire was a staple for kids growing up in the '60s and early '70s. You can still enjoy fake ads on TV comedy shows and YouTube.

But there's an anti-brand movement that takes itself pretty seriously. Given voice by Naomi Klein's *No Logo: Taking Aim at the Brand Bullies* around the turn of the century, a loose confederation of activists, artists, and nihilists are committed to tilting at the windmills of branding. To them, logos are bad, representing an invasion of social space by commercial interests. The most spirited and insane proponents of this ideology sometimes stage violent protests at meetings of world leaders. Others throw pies in the faces of famous people.

Now, in the spirit of full disclosure, I have been a subscriber to *Adbusters*, which is a "culture jammer" magazine that deconstructs and re-mashes corporate images and liturgy. And I sometimes wear a pair of Blackspot sneakers, which are a *nonbrand* brand, if that makes any sense. So I think it's cool to challenge our conception and expectations of brands. That's what this entire book is about.

But the anti-brand movement is distracted by the superficial imagery of brands. They give brands far too much credit: the salient point of public debate shouldn't be the power of brands, but rather their irrelevance. Logos just don't matter. So put a swoosh or globe or smiling TV thing on Internet sites and billboards. Name streets and children after them if you want. The reality is that branding struggles to produce anything measurable other than this detritus that clutters up our lives. Hate brands for their bad art and inane propaganda, but the anti-brand folks actually elevate that which they wish to demote. Business practices matter, not signs.

It's about the business, stupid.

If anything, branding is a sign of how imperfect and vulnerable businesses can be. They blithely go along, allocating some random number to waste on branding each year. Sometimes the expenditure is calculated as nothing more scientific than a percentage of sales that can be written off or, at worst, as a cost of doing business that has no negative impact after that. On the upside, there's always a vague promise of an improvement or benefit to sales, stock price, employee recruiting, or whatever other improved intangibles one wishes for. Brand doesn't hurt anything per se, so why not entertain consumers with crazy videos, produce ever more hilarious TV commercials, fill the Internet with smarter and cuter e-mails, and plaster over every available space in video games, social networking devices, and humanity's collective consciousness?

Brand continues to be *the business corollary to buying a lottery ticket*. It would be laughable if it wasn't such a colossal waste of money.

So maybe there's no impetus for real change; you and I are trying to fix something that isn't broken. Companies might choose to continue to tolerate the anti-brand activities and the inconsistencies of branding, and allow the marketers and their ad agencies to indulge in whatever machinations reward one another. In fact it's likely, primarily because of the force of inertia and habit.

Maybe companies will continue to allocate branding dollars to philanthropy or corporate social responsibility (yes, it's an acronym, CSR, and there's a thriving universe of consultants and agencies ready to spend client money on it), so some of us might briefly think less critically or clearly about businesses that try to attach good-works associations to their brands.

More branding books will be written, more clients will spend money on agencies and media outlets, more awards will be awarded, and more people will trade jobs more often. My modest proposal might not be so modest at all, irrespective of how many visionary companies are embracing it. Tolerating the status quo might be just fine.

But what if consumers chose not to tolerate brands?

I'm not suggesting a mass uprising against consumer culture, or some Luddite nirvana wherein local, handmade commerce has put every aproned Wal-Martian in front of a fiery blacksmith's hearth, potter's wheel, or garden hoe.

Remember when we contemplated in chapter 1 a world without branding? Well, let's imagine a world wherein companies keep branding just the way and as much as they do today.

Let's also imagine that consumers change their behavior further. Ignoring commercials could morph into getting bothered by them. Irritation over online data might become a bigger issue. Entertainment content from companies that should be focused on making whatever it is they sell may actually start to be worrisome to investors and shoppers. The latest pricey investment in a gee-whiz technology promising to overcome some biogenetic resistance to advertising could finally be held accountable, along with the last half-dozen purchases that utterly failed to do the same thing.

The status quo might reveal it has no *quo* anymore.

Here's just a sample of what we could see in the next few years, assuming businesses do nothing to change their approach to brands:

- **Unbrand me, please.** Consumers could just *start saying no* to branding content. Think DVR, e-mail opt-out, social networks without ads, or any number of other ways to refuse or outright avoid marketing. Perhaps we start to see *brand-free zones* where people can aggregate without being bothered or exploited. Places where the most brand messages congregate may become places people ignore, obviating the enormous investment made in online technologies to place ads on websites, which is based on the premise that people will show up to be exposed to them in the first place. What if they choose not to show up as expected?

- **The brand surcharge.** Major, visible investments in glossy brand marketing could become a signal to consumers that a company has lost its way, or is covering up an inadequacy on another front. The most popular branding could be to corporate health what a sports car and trophy second wife are to men's midlife crises. It would be interesting to test whether this is already the case, by tracking the financial performance of businesses that spend a lot of money on branding. Do they return the same profits to investors as those companies without commensurate branding expenditures, and did those results come *from* the branding or occur *in spite* of it?

- **Unbelievable reviews.** The nature of media coverage of businesses could change, as readers and viewers begin to demand something more than the glib "color commentary" that accompanies most marketing announcements. It's just not reasonable for a business journalist to parrot the empty declarations of every corporate communications department that says some expenditure on creative commercials for TV is going to change the way people behave, or do something competitive toward other businesses that's somehow different than what happened last year or the year before that. If the coverage changes, so will our behaviors, and vice versa.

- **No more intangibles.** The free lunch that most branding budgets get from stock analysts may shift if analysts start demanding more statistical proof to support such expenditures. That connection is not necessarily good for brands. Or perhaps the intangibles will become tangible, at risk of losing some of the essence of said values but gaining the benefit of having, well, any value at all. It'll change the IPO and private equity rackets, too.

- **Employee free agency.** The idea that an employee is anything more than a part-time arrangement will find its true realization, as the only reality on which they can depend will be their own behavior. Branding as an idea is irrelevant in the employer-employee relationship unless it's backed by actions, and a new generation of employees who see branding for the empty and irrelevant promise that it is will quickly learn to rely on themselves instead.

- **Cutting out hearts.** The pressures of all of the consumer, media, investor, and employee behaviors will filter back to the marketing department, usually in the form of ever greater performance demands and budget pressures. You can just imagine marketers as initiates of some ancient Mesoamerican priesthood, ripping the hearts out of sacrifices in ever greater numbers, all in hopes of staving off the end of their world. This is how branding strategy could become a bloody mess.

Brand was young last century. Now it's in its midlife crisis.

These changes aren't just possible; based on what's already going on with consumer behavior, it's pretty clear that my imagined world is not an academic exercise.

It's already happening.

Without changes in how we view and deliver brands—fundamental, creative changes that challenge even our most heartfelt truths—we'll still end up in the imaginary world I described in chapter 1, only not because brands have disappeared, but rather because people have just stopped paying attention. Or tolerating them at all.

You need to get ready to operate in a world without branding.

BRING ON THE GOATS

Thank goodness the goat in the centerpiece was already dead.

When back in 2007, journalists arrived at the party to celebrate Sony's much-anticipated video-game sequel, *God of War II*, they found a setting for an ancient Greek bacchanal: nearly naked models served grapes, at least one guy wore a toga, and guests sat amidst goofy decorations and ate meat soup served as if it were bowls of steaming entrails from that dead goat.

There was something to offend everyone at the event, not to forget the video game itself, which was said to be among the most violent in existence.

But it was the goat that did it. The UK's *Daily Mail* picked up the story, the International Fund for Animal Welfare condemned the event, and then the story took off into the blogosphere. Within days, Sony had issued an apology and initiated an internal investigation. This story was picked up by Reuters newswire. More media coverage and blogging ensued.

The story broke through the media clutter. I don't remember another video-game launch that year, or any year, really. For those consumers who already play *God of War*, or might be the sort that would be interested in an über-violent video game, it was all great fun. Many of them wrote blog comments in Sony's defense. I'm sure more than one of them went to the website to check out the new title.

As for those responsible citizens who were offended and spoke out—at least one antiviolence campaigner was quoted in the *Mail* story—they spoke their minds and, in doing so, helped promote the story. The likelihood that any of them would be game buyers after the publicity stunt was no less than what it was before. Parents the world over were probably disgusted, giving the game an extra cool quotient with kids. (The fact that the game is rated Mature, which means kids aren't supposed to be able to buy it, made it even more desirable.)

It was a brilliant guerrilla marketing moment—presuming the marketers at Sony strategized such a grisly prompt for its branding.

They didn't, of course, and it wasn't.

All the Greek trappings, including the goat, were simply *on brand* for the game, which involves characters based on Greek mythology. Sony wasn't trying to offend anyone, and the event was otherwise a total dud, considering coverage of it came *two months after the fact* and only when Sony shipped its *PlayStation* magazine with a two-page spread on the party. Nobody at the actual gig found any of it much worth reporting on. And once the story was revealed to a wider audience, the company did its best to downplay all of the goat-decapitated, blood-pooling, guts-eating, naked-women aspects of the branding that made it worth retelling, or acting upon. In fact, the crisis communications strategy was likely intended to dampen *any* reactions.

Long-term associations with the brand needed to be taken in consideration, of course. The story couldn't just be left "out there." Brand trumped behavior.

Most businesses are still similarly unable to embrace behavior as brand. For every ingenious, smart marketing innovation—not just stuff that's notably gross, but plans that engage people and get them to do things that matter for the business—there are many more activities that evince a greater interest in the vague, esoteric tendencies in people's forebrains. Belief is still widespread that emotional associations and potential for action are hidden inside people; like souls, or a predisposition to binge drink, brands influence our lives more than the actual attributes of experience, or the performance of a purchased product or service.

Every business needs someone, usually an entire department, to spend time and money talking about brands in artistically pleasing images and the hushed, reverent tones that accompany slide presentations. Your business is likely doing it right now.

I say bring on the goats.

It's high time we start seeing and believing in a new, more realistic definition of brand as the behaviors that constitute the real-time give-and-take between, within, and among the people who consume, produce, support, or simply have an interest in a product or service. It's this reality, understood and organized with a broad planning tool called a Chronology of Purchase Intent, that will let businesses use awareness and thought as contributors to meaningful and measurable action.

Brands are so much more than ideas.

Branding in its infancy was enamored with the powers of persuasion and creativity. Now, in its muddled midlife, branding needs to broaden and deepen, to find a basis in behavior, in reality, in science, and, yes, in creativity. We can no longer claim this consensual hallucination is real. It isn't, and brands aren't. We can, however, make branding real and make it matter. We need to start talking about it right now.

Hopefully, *Branding Only Works on Cattle* has helped prompt that conversation. I've tried to take what we marketers talk about behind closed doors and bring it into the light of day. In this process, maybe it has ceased to be a marketing-insider issue and can be seen as solvable by a wider group of individuals. We need the help, as the same old answers, however wrapped in glossy new-media ideas, haven't worked so far. Businesses worldwide are striving to redefine the ways they envision and deliver brands to consumers, and are still being told that they're getting the right answers while they're getting the wrong sales results.

Well, let's start asking new questions.

Remember that we all want to compete better, sell more, and make lots of money. The role brands can and should play in accomplishing those goals is changing, and it's going to change a lot more. When you picked up this book, you opened your eyes to see that the emperor of brands wasn't wearing any clothes.

Now, having finished it, perhaps you agree with me. Perhaps you have better ideas already, or have started or joined a debate about finding new definitions for the branding practiced within your own organization. Maybe you are going to start looking to do something about it tomorrow, or will change something yet today. I doubt you'll ever look the same way again at all the branding nonsense that surrounds us.

If you'd like to talk more and help keep the conversation of this book going, please visit my website, www.baskinbrand.com, or my blog, Dim Bulb, at dimbulb.typepad.com. Let's celebrate what works and debate what doesn't.

Thanks for your time. I hope you've had some fun along the way, throwing wrenches into Ptolemy's fancy gears.

I say we're just getting started.

Notes

Chapter 1: Your Branding Is Useless

1. Russ Klein, president, Global Marketing, Strategy and Innovation, Burger King, as quoted in ANA Marketing Maestros, October 6, 2006. http://ana.blogs.com/maestros/2006/10.

2. Financial estimate compiled from information in a web article by Betsy Spethmann, "Gap Insists Financial Woes Won't Affect Product RED," http://promomagazine.com/retail/news, February 22, 2007, as well as data available on the Gap website, http://www.gap.com.

3. Dim Bulb can be read at http://dimbulb.typepad.com, and there you'll find information on the extra-content podcast.

4. "McDonald's Reports Record Results for 2006," company press release, January 24, 2007, http://www.rmhc.com/corp/news/corppr.html.

5. Spending on brand advertising alone among the "Top 25 US Mega-brands" topped $16 billion, according to *Advertising Age*'s "Fact Pack 2006."

6. There is ample news coverage of the various machinations of branding, such as the AT&T/Cingular expenditure, which undid a branding effort only a few years earlier that may have cost an estimated $1 billion. Laurie J. Flynn, "Goodbye Cingular, Hello to the New Bell, AT&T," *New York Times*, May 21, 2007. The Consignia debacle mirrored that experience, as described by Abram D. Saur, "Consignia: Royal F**k Up," June 24, 2002, http://www.brandchannel.com/features_profile.asp?pr_id=76.

7. In fact, the comedy publication the *Onion* had run a mock news story

eighteen months before the actual launch, suggesting on February 18, 2004, that Gillette would introduce a five-bladed razor simply because, well, it could.

8. Greg Welch, "CMO Tenure: Slowing Down the Revolving Door," a Spencer Stuart blue paper.

9. Roland Marchand, *Creating the Corporate Soul: The Rise of Public Relations and Corporate Imagery in American Big Business* (Berkeley: University of California Press, 1998), 7–41.

10. The Museum of Public Relations, "1929: Torches of Freedom," http://www.prmuseum.com/bernays/bernays_1929.html.

Chapter 2: Traces in a Cloud Chamber

1. *BusinessWeek*, "Here's How We Calculate the Power in a Name," http://images.businessweek.com/ss/06/07/top_brands/index_01.htm, undated; also analyzed Special Report, "The 100 Top Brands," *BusinessWeek*, August 4, 2003, and "Interbrand's Best Global Brands 2006," an Interbrand publication.

2. Kevin Helliker, "This Is Your Brain on a Strong Brand: MRIs Show Even Insurers Can Excite," *Wall Street Journal*, November 28, 2006, B1.

3. "Taste Challenge 'A State of Mind,' " BBC News, October 13, 2004, http://news.bbc.co.uk/2/hi/health/3739462.stm.

4. Elizabeth G. Miller and Barbara E. Kahn, "Shades of Meaning: The Effect of Color and Flavor Names on Consumer Choice," *Journal of Consumer Research* 32 (June 2005).

5. Ian Sample, "The Brain Scan That Can Read People's Intentions," *Guardian* (UK), February 9, 2007.

6. "Researchers Use Brain Scans to Predict When People Will Buy," *Spotlight News*, Carnegie Mellon University feature, January 3, 2007; additional coverage in the *Economist*, January 13, 2007.

7. Michael C. Mozer, Todd Mytkowicz, Richard S. Zemel, "Achieving Robust Neural Representations: An Account of Repetition Suppression," Abstract, Department of Computer Science, University of Colorado, Boulder, 2004.

8. Prashant Malaviya, "The Moderating Influences of Advertising Content on Ad Repetition Effects: The Role of Amount and Type of Elaboration," INSEAD white paper, April 2000, http://knowledge.insead.edu.

9. V. Srinivasan, Chan Su Park, and Dae Ryun Chang, "An Approach to The Measurement, Analysis and Prediction of Brand Equity and Its Sources," *Management Science*, September 2005.

10. You can learn more about Jim's book and consulting practice at http://www.lenskold.com.

Chapter 4: The Rise of the Anti-Brand

1. Emre Sokullu, "Search 2.0—What's Next?" Read/WriteWeb, December 13, 2006, http://www.readwriteweb.com.
2. "The Search for Professional Search," a Convera survey, December 2006, http://knewworld.com.
3. Kate Kaye, "Piper Pegs 2011 web Ad Spending at Over $80 Billion," ClickZ news, February 23, 2007, http://www.clickz.com.
4. Direct magazine, "Search Engines Generate 2.3% Conversion Rate on websites," January 30, 2006, http://directmag.com/news.
5. As William J. McEwen explains in *Married to the Brand: Why Consumers Bond with Some Brands for Life* (Gallup, New York: 2005).
6. "Search Is Brand," white paper by Market Sentinel and Weboptimiser, June 2005, based on a search via Google, www.weboptimiser.com/resources/Searchisbrand280605.pdf.
7. "One of Four Big-Brand Search Links Go to Consumer-Generated Content," MarketingVOX: The Voice of Online Marketing, December 14, 2006, http://www.marketingvox.com.
8. "Search Engine Brand Management," white paper, Hitwise, February 2006, http://www.hitwise.com.
9. "Search Before the Purchase: Understanding Buyer Search Activity as It Builds to Online Purchase," DoubleClick white paper, February 2005, http://www.doubleclick.com.
10. It seems that much of social judgment and behavior happen without conscious awareness or intent, as per John A. Bargh, "Losing Consciousness: Automatic Influences on Consumer Judgment, Behavior, and Motivation," *Journal of Consumer Research* 29 (2002).
11. George Eliot, *Daniel Deronda* (1876), book 6, chapter 42.
12. Jennifer Laycock, "Search Engine Users Head Offline to Shop," Search Engine Guide, January 26, 2005, http://www.searchengineguide.com.
13. Jessica Mintz, "Microsoft Adds Behavioral Targeting," *Las Vegas Sun*, December 27, 2006.
14. Riva Richmond, "Yahoo Ad-Ranking Tool Scores," *Wall Street Journal*, February 28, 2007.
15. Bob Tedeschi, "E-Commerce Report," *New York Times*, November 3, 2003, Sec. C.

16. John Suler, Ph.D, "The Online Disinhibition Effect," *CyberPsychology and Behavior* 7, no. 3 (2004).

17. Juliette Garside, "Mobile Giants Plot Secret Rival to Google," *Sunday Telegraph* (UK), May 2, 2007.

18. Steve Miller, "Saab Accused of Rigging Search Engine Results," *BrandWeek*, January 29, 2007.

19. "Revealed: How eBay Sellers Fix Auctions," *Sunday Times* (London), January 28, 2007.

20. E-mail from Richard Firminger, director of Northern European sales for Yahoo! Search Marketing, as reported in Search Engine Watch, http://blog.searchenginewatch.com, posted by Frank Watson, January 24, 2007.

21. Any recent news item on http://www.scrwire.com; NGOs seem to vie with corporations for trust.

Chapter 5: The Myth of the Consumer/Producer

1. http://brokensaints.com/blog.

2. http://www.xiaoxiaomovie.com.

3. http://www.newvoyages.com.

4. Amanda Lenhart, "User-Generated Content," Pew Internet research, November 6, 2006.

5. http://www.degreemen.com.

6. http://www.bud.tv.

7. Greg Sandoval, "GM Slow to React to Nasty Ads," CNET News, April 3, 2006, http://www.cnet.com.

8. Bazaarvoice press release, citing Yankelovich, Inc., April 2005, http://www.bazaarvoice.com; also Christopher Vollmer, John Frelinghuysen, and Randall Rothenberg, "The Future of Advertising Is Now," Strategy + Business, Special Report, http://www.strategy-business.com.

9. Theresa Howard, "Advertisers Forced to Think Way Outside the Box," *USA Today*, June 19, 2005, http://www.usatoday.com.

10. Read Montague, *Why Choose This Book? How We Make Decisions* (New York: Dutton, 2006), 1–56.

Chapter 6: The Outsourcing of Consent

1. "Get Naked and Rule the World," *Wired* magazine cover story, March 2007.

2. "The 25 Basic Styles of Blogging . . . and When to Use Each One," presentation by Rohit Bhargava and Jesse Thomas, 360 Digital Influence,

a group within Ogilvy Public Relations Worldwide, accessed May 23, 2007.

3. Work at http://www.weblab.org on small group dialogue, or SDG, goes back at least to 1998; reports such as "Changing the Nature of Online Conversation: An Evaluation of RealityCheck.com," February 2000, are very insightful on the subject.

4. Ad Pulp, "Pontiac Finds Innovative Way to Market Cars on MySpace," February 11, 2007, http://www.adpulp.com; Peter Valdes-Dapena, "Real Cars Drive into Second Life," November 18, 2006, http://www.cnn.com.

5. Greg's blog is at http://gregverdino.typepad.com.

6. Apophenia, danah's blog, is at http://www.zephoria.org/thoughts.

7. You can explore some of the conversation at http://deoxy.org/forum/ postlist.pl?Cat=4&Board=mckenna.

Chapter 7: Games as Purpose, Not Distraction

1. "Top 10 Industry Facts," Entertainment Software Association, March 5, 2007, http://www.theesa.com.

2. Chao Xiong, "Where the Girls Are," *Wall Street Journal*, October 28, 2003, sec. B.

3. "The State of the Console," Nielsen Wireless and Interactive Services, Nielsen Company, Fourth Quarter, 2006.

4. Kim Yoon-mi, "Korea: Middle-Aged Users Drive Internet Craze," Asia-Media News Daily, February 2, 2007, http://www.asiamedia.ucla.edu; Michael Kanellos, "South Korea's Digital Dynasty," CNET News, June 25, 2004, http://www.cnet.com.

5. Martha Pitts, "Food Companies Target Online Kids," CFK, July 19, 2006, http://www.connectforkids.org.

6. Jon Wilcox, "Scarface Kills Over Two Million Sales," Total Video Games, May 18, 2007, http://www.totalvideogames.com.

7. *Time* magazine, Style & Design issue, Spring 2007.

Chapter 8: It Takes a Company

1. "Top Ten Complaints," Consumer Direct, January 9, 2007, http://www .consumerdirect.gov.uk.

2. National Consumer Affairs Center of Japan, *NCAC News,* 18, no. 6 (March 2007).

3. Jeremy Kirk, "French Consumer Group Files Complaints Against HP," Network World/IDG News Service, December 15, 2006, http://www .networkworld.com.

4. Allen E. Alter, "Despite IT Support, Customer Service Is Getting Worse," *CIO Insight*, November 21, 2006.

5. "Fourth Quarter, 2006: Retail Trade; Finance & Insurance; E-Commerce," ACSI, February 20, 2007, http://www.theacsi.org.

6. Speakers from those companies and many more were featured at the Asian Six Sigma Summit 2006, June 27–28, 2006, according to http://www.iqpc.com.

7. Scott M. Patton, "Four Days with W. Edwards Deming," W. Edwards Deming Institute, http://www.deming.org, Day One.

8. Peter Kim, "Reinventing the Marketing Organization," independent Forrester Report, July 13, 2006.

9. Edward Tufte, "PowerPoint Is Evil," *Wired*, issue 11.09, September 2003.

10. Rhonda L. Rundle, "Critical Case: How an E-mail Rant Jolted a Big HMO," *Wall Street Journal*, April 24, 2007, sec. A.

Chapter 9: The Buzz in Buzz Marketing

1. "Beyond Café Society: Bring on the Smoothie Wars," *Independent* (UK), April 21, 2007, http://www.enjoyment.independent.co.uk.

2. Lee McEwan, quoting a research paper entitled "Competitive Brands' User Profiles Rarely Differ," by Ehrenberg, Long, and Kennedy, presented at a Market Research Society, 2000, via his blog, "Serendipity Book," http://www.leemcewan.com.

3. http://www.historyofbranding.com.

4. http://www.nintendo.com/corp/history.jsp.

5. Kathleen Pender, "Intuit's Tax-Day Meltdown," *San Francisco Chronicle*, April 19, 2007, http://www.sfgate.com.

6. Thomas D. Seeley and P. Kirk Visscher, "Group Decision Making in Nest-Site Selection by Honey Bees," *Apidologie* 35 (2004), www.apidologie.org.

7. Deborah M. Gordon, "The Organization of Work in Social Insect Colonies," *Complexity*, 8, no. 1 (September 2002); also, *Ants at Work: How an Insect Society Is Organized* (New York: W. W. Norton, 2000).

8. http://www.cultureby.com/trilogy.

Bibliography

Battelle, John. *The Search: How Google and Its Rivals Rewrote the Rules of Business and Transformed Our Culture.* New York: Portfolio, 2005.

Bernays, Edward L. *Propaganda: The Public Mind in the Making.* New York: Liveright Corporation, 1936.

Bligh, Philip, and Douglas Turk. *CRM Unplugged: Releasing CRM's Strategic Value.* Hoboken, NJ: John Wiley & Sons, 2004.

Bohm, David. *Causality and Chance in Modern Physics.* Philadelphia: University of Pennsylvania Press, 1957.

Boorstin, Daniel J. *The Image: A Guide to Pseudo-Events in America.* New York: Atheneum, 1987.

Bourdieu, Pierre. *On Television.* New York: New Press, 1996.

Brown, Jimmy. "Development of a Multi-Dimensional Strategy Model." Ph.D. diss., Benedictine University, 2007. http://www.3cstrategy.com, May 18, 2007.

Brown, John Seely, and Paul Duguid. *The Social Life of Information.* Boston: Harvard Business School Press, 2000.

Brown, Mary, and Carol Orsborn. *Boom: Marketing to the Ultimate Power Consumer—the Baby-Boomer Woman.* New York: AMACOM, 2006.

Cantor, Norman F. *In the Wake of the Plague: The Black Death and the World It Made.* New York: Free Press, 2001.

Castronova, Edward. *Synthetic Worlds: The Business and Culture of Online Games.* Chicago: University of Chicago Press, 2005.

Csikszentmihalyi, Mihaly. *Good Business: Leadership, Flow, and the Making of Meaning*. New York: Viking, 2003.

Edelman, Gerald M., and Giulio Tononi. *A Universe of Consciousness: How Matter Becomes Imagination*. New York: Basic Books, 2000.

Eisenberg, Bryan, Jeffrey Eisenberg, and Lisa T. Davis. *Waiting for Your Cat to Bark? Persuading Customers When They Ignore Marketing*. Nashville: Thomas Nelson, 2006.

Ewen, Stuart. *PR! A Social History of Spin*. New York: Basic Books, 1996.

Freberg, Stan. *Tip of the Freberg: The Stan Freberg Collection 1951–1998*. CD box set. Rhino Entertainment, 1999.

Fuller, R. Buckminster. *Nine Chains to the Moon: An Adventure Story of Thought*. Philadelphia: J. B. Lippincott, 1938.

Gilder, George. *Life After Television: The Coming Transformation of Media and American Life*. New York: Whittle Direct Books, 1990.

Godin, Seth. *Permission Marketing: Turning Strangers into Friends, and Friends into Customers*. New York: Simon & Schuster, 1999.

Gordon, Deborah M. *Ants at Work: How an Insect Society Is Organized*. New York: W. W. Norton, 2000.

Grappone, Jennifer, and Gradiva Couzin. *Search Engine Optimization: An Hour a Day*. Indianapolis: Wiley, 2006.

Herman, Edward S., and Noam Chomsky. *Manufacturing Consent: The Political Economy of the Mass Media*. New York: Pantheon, 1988.

Hill, Dan. *Body of Truth: Leveraging What Consumers Can't or Won't Say*. Hoboken, NJ: John Wiley & Sons, 2003.

Jenkins, Henry. *Convergence Culture: Where Old and New Media Collide*. New York: New York University Press, 2006.

Laermer, Richard, and Mark Simmons. *Punk Marketing: Get Off Your Ass and Join the Revolution*. New York: HarperCollins, 2007.

Lenskold, James D. *Marketing ROI: The Path to Campaign, Customer, and Corporate Profitability*. New York: McGraw-Hill, 2003.

Lessig, Lawrence. *Free Culture: How Big Media Uses Technology and the Law to Lock Down Culture and Control Creativity*. New York: Penguin, 2004.

Lippmann, Walter. *Public Opinion*. New Brunswick, NJ: Transaction, 1998.

Lynch, Aaron. *Thought Contagion: How Belief Spreads Through Society; The New Science of Memes*. New York: Basic Books, 1996.

McCracken, Grant. *Flock and Flow: Predicting and Managing Change in a Dynamic Marketplace*. Bloomington: Indiana University Press, 2006.

McKenna, Terence. *The Archaic Revival: Speculations on Psychedelic Mushrooms, the Amazon, Virtual Reality, UFOs, Evolution, Shamanism, the Rebirth of the Goddess, and the End of History*. New York: HarperSanFrancisco, 1991.

McLuhan, Marshall. *The Mechanical Bride: Folklore of Industrial Man.* New York: Vanguard, 1951.

————*Understanding Media: The Extensions of Man.* Cambridge, MA: MIT Press, 1995.

Manchester, William. *A World Lit Only by Fire: The Medieval Mind and the Renaissance: Portrait of an Age.* New York: Little, Brown, 1992.

Marchand, Roland. *Creating the Corporate Soul: The Rise of Public Relations and Corporate Imagery in American Big Business.* Berkeley: University of California Press, 1998.

Minsky, Marvin. *The Emotion Machine: Commonsense Thinking, Artificial Intelligence, and the Future of the Human Mind.* New York: Simon & Schuster, 2006.

Montague, Read. *Why Choose This Book? How We Make Decisions.* New York: Dutton, 2006.

Morville, Peter. *Ambient Findability.* Sebastopol, CA: O'Reilly Media, 2005.

Neumeier, Marty. *The Brand Gap: How to Bridge the Distance Between Business Strategy and Design.* Berkeley, CA: New Riders, 2006.

Olins, Wally. *Corporate Identity: Making Business Strategy Visible Through Design.* Boston: Harvard Business School Press, 1989.

Ostroff, Frank. *The Horizontal Organization: What the Organization of the Future Actually Looks Like and How It Delivers Value to Customers.* New York: Oxford University Press, 1999.

Packard, Vance. *The Waste Makers.* New York: Pocket, 1963.

Popkin, Jeremy D., ed. *Media and Revolution.* Lexington: University Press of Kentucky, 1995.

Porter, Michael E. *Competitive Strategy: Techniques for Analyzing Industries and Competitors.* New York: Free Press, 1998.

Ramachandran, V. S. *A Brief Tour of Human Consciousness.* New York: Pi, 2004.

Reisterer, Tim, and Diane Emo. *Customer Message Management.* Mason, OH: Texere, 2006.

Robertson, Donald W. *The Mind's Eye of Buckminster Fuller.* New York: St. Martin's, 1974.

Roszak, Theodore. *The Cult of Information: A Neo-Luddite Treatise on High-Tech, Artificial Intelligence, and the True Art of Thinking.* Berkeley: University of California Press, 1994.

Rushkoff, Douglas. *Get Back in the Box: How Being Great at What You Do Is Great for Business.* New York: Collins, 2007.

Sernovitz, Andy. *Word of Mouth Marketing: How Smart Companies Get People Talking.* Chicago: Kaplan, 2006.

Sidgwick, Eleanor M. *Phantasms of the Living: Cases of Telepathy Printed in the Journal of the Society of Psychical Research During Thirty-five Years.* New Hyde Park, NY: University Books, 1962.

Standage, Tom. *The Victorian Internet: The Remarkable Story of the Telegraph and the Nineteenth Century's On-Line Pioneers.* New York: Walker, 1998.

Sterling, Bruce. *Shaping Things.* Cambridge, MA: MediaWork/MIT Press, 2005.

Strogatz, Steven. *SYNC: The Emerging Science of Spontaneous Order.* New York: Hyperion, 2003.

Sutton, Dave, and Tom Klein. *Enterprise Marketing Management: The New Science of Marketing.* Hoboken, NJ: John Wiley & Sons, 2003.

Thompson, William I. *The American Replacement of Nature: the Everyday Acts and Outrageous Evolution of Economic Life.* New York: Currency/Doubleday, 1991.

Travis, Daryl. *Emotional Branding: How Successful Brands Gain the Irrational Edge.* New York: Crown Business, 2000.

Trow, George W. S. *Within the Context of No Context.* New York: Atlantic Monthly Press, 1997.

Tybout, Alice M., and Tim Calkins, eds. *Kellogg on Branding.* Hoboken, NJ: John Wiley & Sons, 2005.

Tye, Larry. *The Father of Spin: Edward L. Bernays and the Birth of Public Relations.* New York: Crown, 1998.

Wilson, Edward O. *Consilience: The Unity of Knowledge.* New York: Alfred A. Knopf, 1998.

Winter, Alison. *Mesmerized: Powers of Mind in Victorian Britain.* Chicago: University of Chicago Press, 1998.

Index

About the Author

JONATHAN SALEM BASKIN has decades of experience translating branding strategy into something more than images and words, working with Apple, Blockbuster, ConAgra, and many of the other companies that make up the brand-name alphabet. Combined with an education that ranges from medieval computer arts to cut-up romantic poetry, his perspective on branding is the first to incorporate business accountability and efficiency, creativity, and a commitment to the premise that the best way to discover better answers consistently is to ask better questions relentlessly.

You can join the conversation at http://www.baskinbrand.com and enjoy his Dim Bulb raves on the most fantastic and foolish in brand marketing each day at http://dimbulb.typepad.com. When he's not writing, Jonathan leads a global consultancy, working with clients in North America, Europe, and Asia. In an alternate life, he was a rock star.